I KNOW IT WAS THE BLOOD:
A STORY OF OVERCOMING

BY CEOLA J. ABRAM

I Know It Was the Blood:A Story of Overcoming!
by Ceola J. Abram

Printed in the United States of America.
Edited by Xulon Press

ISBN 9781498475792

Unless otherwise indicated, Scripture quotations are taken from the King James Version (KJV) – public domain

www.xulonpress.com

TABLE OF CONTENTS

Introduction

"For whatsoever is born of God overcometh the world:
and this is the victory that overcometh the world,
even our faith."

1 John 5:4

This was a very hard book to write because it required me to be transparent. Over fifteen years ago, the Lord told me transparency is the bridge that builds trust. At the time he said this to me, I had no idea what this meant, nor did I have any clue as to what it would mean to me and the many others the Lord would lead me to later on in my life.

Revealing your inner and darkest secrets is a very difficult task. Doing so not only makes you a target for judgement, but for a plethora of gossip. It also makes you vulnerable, and if you're not careful, and you don't know who you are in Christ Jesus, it places you at the mercy of others. I struggled long and hard with this assignment, but I knew it was part of my journey of life with God.

Sharing information with the entire world that only a handful of people know is a huge leap of faith—or the most foolish and stupid thing I have ever done thus far! The difference in the two is the why behind the what. My "why" is God and the "what" is the obedience, trust, hope, and faith I have chosen to put in God as I take this journey with Him.

My prayer is that most readers of this book will look beyond my faults and resist the temptation to judge and/or condemn me, but rather to see the story as one offering inspiration, encouragement, and motivation through a heart of compassion. I would hope it is seen as an opportunity given by God to find hope and grasp his unfailing and merciful love through the redemptive blood of Jesus Christ.

We all need the love of God and the saving grace of Jesus Christ. Perhaps through this book, God will tear down the walls of division we as women have built against one another through the same forgiving spirit he has shared with us through our Lord and Savior Jesus Christ. None of us are perfect! We all have skeletons in our closet—all of us. The only difference between you and me is that God has instructed me to throw my closet door wide open and share my story. In doing so, I have been liberated, and I believe those who read this book will find liberty as well. Your liberty will not be found through me, or my words, but through Jesus Christ and the shedding of his blood, and the unconditional love of God. The story I share testifies to the power of the blood. A story of a yielded vessel, surrendered to my Lord; one who has overcome by the very words of my testimony and by the blood of the lamb.

I pray if you choose to purchase and read this book, that you would pray before you open the pages and ask God to first help you not to see me, but to see him. Ask him to allow your spirit to be receptive, for your heart to be open, and your spiritual ears to be tuned to hear what "thus says the Lord."

Thank you,

Ceola

Acknowledgements

I would like to say a huge thank you to my grandmother, Wilma Jean Buck. She has been my ROCK all my life. She is the person who taught me about God, Jesus and the Holy Spirit, and how to live a Christian life. She is the person who would tell me stories of her father, my great-grandfather, who was a minister who traveled per request to various tent meetings to heal the sick. She has told me many stories over the years; stories that have encouraged me in the gospel and have helped me through some pretty rough passages in life. It is the stories she told me over the years that have challenged me to seek more knowledge of Jesus Christ. I will never forget the times we spent talking as she shared stories with me about my lineage, about my heritage.

It was my grandmother who always encouraged me to stay in church and to put God first in all things. Whenever I would find myself in challenging situations, she would always remind me to pray and that God would not fail me. No matter where we found ourselves, her faith was always "I put my trust in God." That was—and is to this day—her response to every situation. She is my go-to spiritual advisor; the times I spent with her were the most influential in my life. She is the most amazing role model any young girl/woman could ever have asked for. It seems only fitting for me to acknowledge her.

She has demonstrated before all of "her daughters" as she calls us, how to be ladies. In her, we saw real strength, poise, class, and elegance. She showed us a great example of how a lady should be treated by how she lived. She never accepted less than what she was deserving of as a woman of God. She is a woman who knew her worth. It's because of the life she lived before me that I am the lady I am today. Mistakes and bad decisions I made have no reflection on her grooming me. In fact, I was only able to overcome as a result of how solidly she lived before me. By how her faith in God seemed to pull her through her own obstacles. It's not that she escaped the clinches of life's trials and tribulations, it's because of her faith in God that she triumphed over them and my victories are certainly attributed to the faith she demonstrated before me and as a result, I too have been triumphant. Thank you, Granny Granny! I love you more than my words could ever articulate. I AM YOUR TWIN and it's a title I wear with great honor.

Lorraine Lewis (Rainy), I cannot even begin to express in mere words what our friendship has meant to me in the last few years. It amazes me that we have only known each other for a short period of time. It seems like years of fun, fellowship, prayer, laughter, tears and excitement about the future. You have truly shown me what it means to be a true friend and for that I will be forever grateful to you. I thought I was too old to stay on the phone with someone for long periods of time, but talking with you about God, the vision, our personal stuff, laughing and sometimes crying, but in all giving praises to God, has been awesome. You ARE truly a blessing sent directly from God and oh, how I thank Him for you daily! Love you, girl!

Mrs. Pamela Dobson (aka Mama Pam) what words can I say about such a beautiful Godly woman as you. It's amazing to me, but from the first time we met, you captured my heart. While my beloved mother can never be replaced, you have come amazingly close. You can't tell me what God can't do. You have been there for me in difficult times, always availing yourself. You have encouraged me, you have comforted me and on occasion, you have even debated with me. You have cried with me, you have laughed with me and supported me without fail and in your own cute way, I've seen you defend me, and you have gladly and humbly assisted me. I love how you will call me and sing me a worship or praise song and then do your "SOS" prayer. I love you with all of my heart lady and I pray we have up until your one-hundred and twentieth birthday to be in each other's lives. I know; you're living to be one hundred and twenty years old. That makes me live to be around one-hundred years old. I thank God for you and your incredible gift to love as God himself loves.

Prophetess Alicia Brown, I can't thank you enough for your help and understanding of the Prophetic call on my life. The first day we spoke revealed a lot about who you were as a person. Since that conversation, your impact on my life has been such a blessing. It's been said by more than a few, there's a call on my life, but you were the one who so lovingly, yet strongly removed my training wheels when I wanted to scurry to the back out of fear of what people would say or think. Sharing our very similar experiences helped me to realize I wasn't crazy, nor was I the ONLY one. When a TRUE Prophet enters your life, a shift is guaranteed! *"Surely the Lord GOD will do nothing, but he revealeth his secret unto his servants the prophets"* (Amos 3:7). Thank you for your obedience, love, support, and sisterhood!

James Kimo Rodriguez, I don't know where you are at the writing of this book, but I often think of you. The time you would take out every morning to share the gospel of Jesus Christ with me will never be forgotten.

All of the books, cassette tapes (funny), and pamphlets you gave me—along with the many chats we would have sitting by your locker about how God loved me and what Jesus did for me—I will forever cherish. You were my guardian angel and I will never forget how you called me "Little One." Your words and amazing love for God and his people inspire me to this day. You had such a pure heart and an incredible love for our Lord and Savior, something that is truly rare today. As I sit writing this section of the book, I can still see your bearded face with that welcoming smile walking the warehouse floors in your freezer suit. I pray wherever you are you know how much I love you and appreciate you for every prayer and word you spoke to me and over me that has helped to shape my life. I know you were a very integral part of the very call on my life. Every person I've had the opportunity to share the gospel of our Lord and Savior is done with thanks to you! Thank you for your faithfulness to God and the many prayers I know you prayed for me. I will always love you Kimo, Little One!

To my mother and father in-law, Wallace and Beverly Tarver, you two are constantly on my mind. I am always thinking of how I want to bless your socks off! I cannot thank you enough for your love and your unwavering support. There are so many words I want to say, but it would require writing another book to express my heart and to share my overwhelming gratitude to you both. My heart desires to do a wonderful thing for you both and I trust God will grant me the opportunity to do so. With all of my love, I say thank you!

To the coolest father-in-law ever, Carl Lee Abram, Sr. I appreciate your love, support, and honesty. Thank you for being there and for offering great words of wisdom when I needed them most. There is something comforting when words of wisdom are spoken from a father. Thank you for accepting me as your daughter-in-law and for always being available. With a heart of gratitude, Thank you!

To my wonderful husband, Carl Lee Abram, Jr. what can I say about you, love? It's pretty incredible that after years of friendship, running into each other, and helping each other when needed, we would find ourselves married to each other. I am Mrs. Carl Lee Abram, Jr. Our friendship, marriage, and history have further shown me that God is ever-so-merciful, forgiving, redeeming, and that he is a father above all. When we missed the mark, humbled ourselves, repented, and chose to obey God, he placed us back on the path to righteousness according to His good and perfect will. That road my not have been an easy one, but I am glad we stayed the course together.

For thirty-plus years now you have been my best friend. We've laughed together, cried together and sat and talked for hours on end together. Thank you for your willingness to put your trust in me, even when it was challenging for us. Many laughed and talked about the steps of obedience that were being taken, the journey that we were on, criticized the choices and decisions that were being made, but look Carl—just look at what God can, has, and continues to do. Trust me when I say our eyes have yet to see all that God has in store for us. Mark my words, honey, God is a restorer and this is just the beginning of promises yet to be fulfilled! As long as we stay the course, remain obedient and faithful to God and God alone, and if our hearts stay directed towards the people of God with outstretched hands and hearts of true and sincere compassion, we will experience the continued beauty of God! God is faithful to the faithful! Watch and see. His promises are *Yes* and *Amen*. With all my heart, your wife!

There are so many more that I would like to acknowledge who mean just as much to me as those aforementioned persons. Your lives have had much impact on me over the years and I love you all so very much. You are in my very small circle of friends whose love, support, and friendship have been the wind beneath my wings, and without whom I could not have survived.

To Barbara Fulcher, you have been my best friend since 1991. No words could ever express the love I have for you. Together we have seen and triumphed through much, even embarking on the path back to God; a journey I will never forget. To Rosemary Williams, we met by what some would call a fluke, but we know it was divinely orchestrated. I will never forget our first meeting at MiMi's and how we sat and cried when we realized our dreams were similar. In a short space of time we covered much ground together and we were there for each other through some of life's most difficult times. I am so grateful God allowed us to create wonderful memories, forge a solid friendship and a sisterhood that is not seasonal, but eternal! I love you, girlie! To Mother Rosemary Saffold, from the first time God instructed me to join the "Igniters of the Fire" prayer line at 5:30 a.m. one Thursday morning, you had my heart! You have such fire and zeal and a passion for God that is incredibly infectious and amazing to experience.

I was looking for realness, people who genuinely love and TRUST GOD; everyone at God's Team International, Inc. has the God factor. Thank you for lovingly welcoming me into your family. Pastor Donald A. Jackson, Jr. (Pastor J) and Brother Mark White, you have both shown me and my husband what being a true Pastor and brother of the church is supposed to be. You both have shown us that being "real" saints is about serving, regardless of your titles. We've watched you both give of yourselves freely to those with whom God has entrusted you. It's rather refreshing to see a Pastor really helping people outside of the pulpit. Thank you as well, Pastor J, for recognizing and seeing the gift in me and for being obedient to God, licensing me, and allowing me the freedom to minister in your pulpit as the Spirit of God moves. Brother Mark, I have never seen anyone who loves people the way you do. You are the epitome of what God's people should be like. Your love and willingness to help people is so beautiful to witness. I know God is proud to call you his child. Keep availing yourself to God, through you both, His people are being well taken care of. God's rich blessings upon you both!

To my lovely and beautiful sister, Jackie Jefferson. Our eyes first met in class at the Living Word Institute; we did not know that God had connected us then, but he did. You truly are my Ladybug and I know God will reward the kindness you have shown me. Your heart is beautiful and my heart has been blessed by your friendship, your love, and our sisterly bond. I draw from the moments we spend in worship and fellowship. I love you!

To Minister True Lafayette, you are a rare find my beloved sister. When someone is willing to lay down their life for you, it's a rare and precious jewel. I thank God for you daily, and I know you don't know this, but now you do—as does the entire world! Our times are rare, but powerful and precious. God connected us and our bond is not seasonal, but eternal. I love you with all of my heart and I am ever so grateful for the sisterhood and friendship God has given me in you.

Last, but certainly not least, my dear sister who came back into my life after 30 years. You can't tell me God is not strategic in what he does. Ms. Valencia McKinley, what words do I have for you, my love? God connected us as children and only He knew how vital our connection would become. We needed each other back then and, as a result, we are true sisters today. The bond that was established back then is still breathing life into us today. Reconnecting with you was a refreshing blessing and when I think about you and the times we shared, my heart rejoices at how God so perfectly orchestrates our lives. He cares for us so much that He gave us what we needed in each other. I love you more than you know!

To all of my brothers, my sister, and my brother-in-law—Anthony, Hochi, Jerrick, Shawn, Kevin, Jason, and Sherrie—thank you for your unfailing love, support, and encouragement. It has meant more than words can say. I am happy to have you in my life. We have shared wonderful times and created some beautiful memories together and I look forward to creating even more! Your lives have had a significant impact on me over the years and I love you all so very much. It is an honor to pray for each of you and I trust that God will continually and richly bless you abundantly! With all my heart, Sis!

Dedications

First I would like to dedicate this book to my parents, William M. Robinson and Devoria Johnson (Swift). Even though they have passed on, they are still very much alive in me. I see traits of them both in me and I am reminded daily of their existence. I will forever love and cherish them both. Life may not have turned out the way I desired—having them both here with me—but I am most grateful for the time God allowed me to have with each of them. With these words, I desire to express my unconditional and eternal love for my parents, who have both made their transition.

I would also like to dedicate this book to women worldwide who have overcome victoriously and to those who will look to this book to garner the strength and encouragement to triumph. We are all overcomers according to the living word of God *"For whatsoever is born of God overcometh the world: and this is the victory that overcometh the world, even our faith"* (1 John 5:4). It doesn't matter if it was verbal, sexual, mental, or emotional abuse. It doesn't matter if it was drugs, alcohol, sex, shopping, or any other form of addiction. Regardless of whether it was adultery, prostitution, promiscuity, lying, cheating, gossiping, or anger management issues.

You can overcome a 400 credit score; losing one, two, or three homes, cars, and jobs; being cheated on; suffering a divorce; or being hurt by a friend, Christian brother, sister, or a church family. If you've lost a loved one, grown up without a parent, or were unable to become a parent. Regardless of what it currently is, or was, the Father said we overcame "him"—any and all tactics of the enemy by the Blood of the Lamb and the Words of their (our) testimony (Revelations 12:11).

I would also like to dedicate this book to my Sister, Myisha Lashon Johnson. To me, you are the epitome of an overcomer. I have painfully watched you go from my baby sister, who I fought for in the projects of LA and chased up the stairs in anger over something you did, to helping you with school projects, chaperoning your school events, and becoming a young mother, to quitting school and struggling on many levels.

What I am AMAZINGLY proud to attest to today is that you are indeed AN OVERCOMER. You are a prayer that God answered. Over the past two years, I have watched you bud into the beautiful woman of God I always knew you had the potential to be and God is not finished with you yet. You are a beautiful caterpillar on your journey to becoming a beautiful butterfly. You are on the path to living the life God created you to live, a life with no blemish of what and where you've been. I bless and PRAISE HIS HOLY NAME. I share what I share freely because you, yourself, have shared so freely in hopes that more women would come to know the saving grace and ever-so-merciful God that has brought you through victoriously. You're an inspiration to many and through your life, God has shown what the enemy meant for bad, he alone has turned around and is using it to his glory.

As I have always told you, Sis, you are my BIGGEST HERO. I love you with all of my heart and soul, and as long as I have breath, I will always be your biggest supporter! I love you!

To all of my sisters—Denise King, Sonya Tolliver, and Whitney Robinson—and to all of my spiritual sisters around the world, I dedicate this book to you, too. I want you to know that through the sharing of my story, I have overcome, and that it was ONLY by the Blood of the Lamb and by the Word of my testimony that I did. I want you to know that you, too, can overcome. Be encouraged as you read this book. See yourself in the pages; see your own experiences as you take this journey with me through my life. Look for God in these pages, as I am able to share with you through the Holy Ghost, the Word that I know was working in and throughout all of my life. I want you to know and understand that it is the same Word that can, will, and is working in your life. *"Jesus Christ the same yesterday, and today, and forever"* (Hebrews 13:8 KJV).

I want you to know you CAN overcome the enemy, just as God said in Revelations 12:11, *"by the Blood of the Lamb and by the Word of your testimony."* Don't have the rocks to cry out on your behalf. Open your mouth and, as my grandmother used to say, "Tell the truth and shame the devil." The word of God says in John 8:32, *"And you shall know the truth and the truth shall make you free."* It's sad how the enemy will always come with a counterfeit word and say things like "the truth hurts." The Truth only hurts when we refuse to accept it. Accept the truth from the Father and be made free. Then open your mouth and overcome by sharing how and what the Father liberated you from. Amen! You ARE an OVERCOMER. The Father Said you ARE!

Chapter One

Why?

"But he that knew not, and did commit things worthy of stripes, shall be beaten with few stripes. For unto whomsoever much is given, of him shall be much required: and to whom men have committed much, of him they will ask the more."

Luke 12:48

Truly Laid On My Heart by God

To tell the truth, I have never desired to share my story with anyone, let alone write a book. This is truly something laid on my heart by God. Although God had given me the title of this book close to eight years ago, I didn't seriously start writing the book until September of 2013. Here's how it all came about. In 2011, after completing the first website for the nonprofit organization I had just incorporated, I was adding the staff bios to our website. When writing my own bio, I felt a strong nudge to include a little bit about my childhood. It was my childhood that provoked my desire to open what I described as a home-less shelter for women and children. The more I wrote about my childhood, the more emotionally challenging it became; the information I felt led to share was becoming more in-depth. I thought to myself, "what is God doing?"

As I continued to write, the tears began to fall. It was as if I was transported back into those very moments of my life. When I finished writing, I found myself staring through my tears at a full page of information that included specific details about my mother, details I had never before shared. I felt the same pain I had experi-enced then, including the pain of those who were in my life during that time. Let me tell you, feeling someone else's pain is one of the strangest things you will ever experience. I felt as if I was grieving all over again; that's when I had an epiphany. I felt God telling me, "what you experienced during these specific times in your life is what many other women and children are experiencing now, and what some will experience later. Your testimony will offer hope. What I've done for you and others, I will also do for them." I will NEVER FORGET that experience as long as I live!

After this experience, I was asked to be a guest speaker on an international prayer call. I was asked if I would share information about the nonprofit I had started. I thought this is going to be easy. I had planned to share the mission statement of the nonprofit; it pretty much said it all, and then I would simply answer the questions anyone had, right? Nope, not so at all. As the time drew close for me to share information about the nonprofit, I felt God nudging me to share what I had written in my bio from our website. This can't be. Doesn't he know how private I am? Isn't he aware of how sensitive this information is? Surely, he knows most people will likely judge both me and my mother, right? This couldn't be what God is asking me to do. Clearly, there is a problem with my reception; I cannot be hearing God correctly.

I am a very private person and I did not feel comfortable sharing such private and intimate details about my life. Even though I had already written a full page on our website, I had not published the site. So, technically, it was not visible to anyone and I had full control over what was seen. Did you catch that, "I had full control" . . . that's funny, huh? That was my first mistake: thinking I had any control over my life. However, sharing this information live on an international prayer call was a horse of a different color, and did not offer such "unpublished" protection. I knew once it was shared on this call, it was out there! Not that I had issues of trust with those on the call, not at all. My issue was that it would become public knowledge and no longer under my so-called protection.

The information I was being asked to share brought back all the painful experiences and deeply buried memories from my past, and I personally had no intentions of resurrecting them. I didn't want wounds I had closed to be reopened again. The entire idea of sharing this information simply made me feel uncomfortable. I felt like I had already taken what I thought was a huge step by sharing my bio on an unpublished website, and in my opinion, this was enough sharing. At the thought of publishing the website I felt vulnerable and open to the surety of what I had convinced myself would be judgement, condemnation and a plethora of gossip. None, of which I desired to experience.

WHY?

Why would God want me to do this live? Then again, why would he want me to share private information in writing a book? Maybe this was the first step towards writing the actual book. Maybe this was, shall we say, the ice-breaker in my writing; my opportunity to get my feet wet, so to speak. At this point, I'm feeling like my faith and trust is being super tested by God in asking me to open myself up and share this period of my life. Did I not consider writing a book would be even more in depth? In all honesty, I really hadn't considered it.

Remember, I had no desire to write a book in the first place. If I can be truthful, when God first gave the title, well, I thought it was cute. I didn't take it serious. I'm just being truthful. You know how we do, when God gives a word it comes with excitement and bragging rights. Initially, most of us just talk the talk (brag about the word we received) and the word really never takes flight because it requires something of us to move forward with a word of God. With this attitude, I never once thought about the content of the book. I didn't really believe I was going to be writing a book. It seemed REALLY far-fetched. Me, an author? Get outta here. I simply did not consider it at all.

As the time went on, I was trying to figure out a way to get around sharing what I knew God was asking me to share on this call. Finally, the morning of the 5:30 am call was here and yes, I was still trying to figure out how to get around sharing this information. I was sweating profusely as the clock continued to tick closer to the 5:30 am mark. God had not given me anything else to share, and I knew my plan of sharing the mission statement was not going to fly. My palms were sweating and I was nauseated. I was a hot mess, and that darn clock would not stop ticking!

When the facilitator of the call introduced me I thought I was going to pass out. There are women on this call from all over and you could sense the expectation. Not because of me, but because of the reputation the facilitator had of having powerfully anointed guest speakers on this call. I thought to myself, surely, I am not in this class of folks. I thought for sure the facilitator had made a major mistake in asking me to be a guest speaker.

I had the pleasure of being on this call before and I knew how serious this group was when it came to God, prayer and a mighty movement of His Holy Spirit. God had to bring his A game or I was certainly going to flop. Due to the mounting pressure I brought upon myself, I thought the surest way to sail smoothly through this call was to obey and do what God asked me to. I cleared my throat and with a slight tremble in my voice and a belly full of nerves, I introduced myself "Good morning, my name is Ceola Abram." I thanked the facilitator and proceeded to tell the audience I was going to share my story. A story I had just written for our website and that this story is where the nonprofit was born from.

As I read the story again, I begin to once again experience the pain of my past. When I finished reading my bio from the website and the lines were open for comments, the women were not slow in sharing their comments. I found it to be amazing what we all had in common. We all thanked God for what he alone had done. It was on this call where I realized again, my story is the story of many women from all walks of life. My tears are the tears of many. I realized when one of us leaps over fear and opens up and shares what God has done in our lives, it frees others to open up as well.

That morning on the prayer line, there was a powerful move of God and with it came a release, needed revelation, and fresh liberty, and it was all so very amazing to experience! From this experience alone, I now had an understanding of the book title "*I Know It Was the Blood: A Story of Overcoming.*" I no longer thought the idea of writing a book was cute. I now knew this was serious and

God was not playing! To this day I know the facilitator may have no idea what God did for me on the prayer call that Thursday morning. I have never shared this story with her or anyone for that matter. That morning when the call ended, I was amazed at what God alone had done. From this experience I learned to further trust God and to be willing and obedient—even when I'm scared. Even when I don't understand and even when I feel unworthy of what I think he's doing in my life. I have come to understand that God knows exactly what he is doing! To everything there is a plan, a purpose and a season. And so it begins: "*I Know It Was the Blood: A Story of Overcoming!*" God's timing is both impeccable and unmatched.

And the Writing Continues

Well, a few years later as noted above I started writing the book. Like I am sure many other first time and maybe even seasoned authors may have felt, I questioned, doubted and experienced the fear of what people would think. Not only of me writing a book, but of what I was going to be potentially sharing. I was really, really concerned about the information I was going to be sharing. I was worried about what my siblings, family and friends would all think. Oh yes, I went through it all, and as a result I would start writing and then stop, start writing again and then stop. Then, one Sunday morning at church, the message was on "Finishing What You Start" and in the message it was said, "God said he was where we left him and to go back and finish what we started last year."

One of the things the Bishop mentioned was the book you started. Have you ever had that moment where you felt like God was talking directly to you and ONLY YOU? That's what I felt like. I wanted to slide down in the pew; I just couldn't figure out how to do it without being noticed. A week after hearing this word from God, I attended Prophetess Alicia Brown's book signing for her book "*Wives on the Wall: 365 Prayers and Declarations for Wives to Pray for Their Husbands.*" She is an anointed Minister, Prophetess, and woman of God and before she got started, she stated firmly, "Every book in the belly would come forth!" With both of these messages I knew God was clearly talking to me! It was time to stop playing and to get serious about writing the book. No more starting and stopping!

Then, just in case I wasn't sure God was strongly beckoning me to seriously start writing, I received an email from a reputable Christian publishing company a few days after the book signing. The subject line read: "A Special Offer on Publishing Your First Book." It was addressed to "First Time Authors" and to this day I have NO idea how they attained my personal email address. Now I know this was a mass email and I know there are ways companies reach their target audience. However, I also knew with the series of recent events God was talking directly to me—LOUD and CLEAR, I might add. As if that was not enough, I received a specific email addressed directly to me from one of the account managers from the SAME publishing company and I thought to myself, okay Father, I get it. So, here I am, beginning to write again.

My Desire Is This

I earnestly pray that through my life's experiences, each reader will see that God has given me a passion for women and children. He has given me a conviction of compassion for women and children; one that burns deep inside of me. I want to share my story of overcoming so others will be encouraged to truly know that if God did it for me, he would do it for them, too. I want all women, no matter where they find themselves, to know they are overcomers, too. I want all women to know we have more in common than we may care to admit and that God is faithful NO MATTER what we've done, or where we may have found ourselves. God's Word says in Romans 8:38-39 *"For I am persuaded, that neither death, nor life, nor angels, nor principalities, nor powers, nor things present, nor things to come, nor height, nor depth, nor any other creature, shall be able to separate us from the love of God, which is in Christ Jesus our Lord."* God is so loving and merciful and we ARE ALL overcomers!

As I sit here writing the beginning of this book for probably the eighth time, I feel as though I am still in the process of overcoming. I know some may wonder how I can be writing a book on overcoming, when I myself may still be in the process of overcoming. Here's how: the process of overcoming does not negate victory. As long as we continue to live this life, we will always be in the midst of overcoming something! The story I share is my account of the things I have overcome up to the point of writing this book. As believer's in Jesus Christ we know we are victorious, right? We know the adversary has already been defeated, right? We know we've endured, persevered and triumphed. Ultimately we know the battle has been won, and we know we're the winners, right?

Through the Blood of Jesus

Through the blood of Jesus Christ, we have been redeemed and placed back in right standing with our Heavenly Father. We've been placed back on course to pursue and to live our lives to the fullest and to finish our race and to do so victoriously. Lamentations 3:22–24 says, *"It is of the LORD's mercies that we are not consumed, because his compassions fail not. They are new every morning: great is thy faithfulness. The LORD is my portion, saith my soul; therefore, will I hope in him."* Although I am writing from a place of overcoming many things over many years, there will be even more "opportunities" for overcoming. The scripture above speaks to the Lord's great mercies, his compassions that fail not, that are new every morning. It is in this that I can continue the course because if he did it before, he will do it again. We have the promise of his word and we know his promises are yes and amen!

From a child it seems as though my life has been in some sort of wild, whirlwind, with many ups, downs, shifts and changes in-between. It would be October of 2014 when yet another shift would come. I was asked to care for my grandmother and aunt and as a result I left my job at a healthcare organization to be home with them and provide the care needed. From October 2014 to May 2015, my grandmother had been hospitalized five times, the dementia was getting worse, and as a result of side effects from one of her medications, she lost the mobility of her legs.

Anyone who has been the care taker of an elderly person knows what all of this means. Talk about a dramatic lifestyle change. All of sudden, there was no sleep, a series of doctor's appointments, frequent visits from nurses, home health aides, occupational therapist and physical therapists. There were also frequent visits to the pharmacy, the ordering of medical supplies and medical equipment. In addition, I am now preparing three meals per day, with diuretic restrictions, an increase in my laundry duties, monitoring blood pressure, sugar levels and weight on a daily basis. This does not include the daily personal hygiene care that is needed.

With the addition of caring for my grandmother, my "other" ministry responsibilities did not cease. I was still writing two blogs, three newsletters, this book, and programs for our nonprofit, as well as maintaining and writing material for six websites. I was designing the marketing material for the nonprofit organization, ministering on some Sundays (yes, in the pulpit), supporting a few young women, and helping individuals and entrepreneurs with their businesses. It was also during this time that the second session of our SPF-90-Day Encouragement Program (a health & wellness program) for our nonprofit began. It was also right in the heat of planning for our second annual women's conference. Oh, and did I mention my "first" ministry, my beloved husband whom I love dearly. I needed to spend time with him, attend to his needs of my company and attention. I am being spread very thin and I still need to run my household. My chores in terms of cleaning my home, washing our laundry, managing our bills, grocery shopping, etc., did not cease. Trust me, I was not as consistent in doing them, but they were done. Bless God!

All of this could not have come at a worse time for me and my husband. It had already been a pretty rough ride for us as we experienced all kinds of challenges: marital challenges, health challenges, financial challenges, etc. If it were not my life, I would not believe this story myself if someone else were telling it. It would seem too unreal and overly dramatized. However, since I'm the one who lived it, I can tell you it's as real as it gets and I dare not tell you everything else that was going on less I run the risk of sounding truly pessimistic. You might be asking why I started off sharing with you what might have come off as both complaining and perhaps some boasting. Let me assure you, my above statements are neither.

Talk About the Blood

When we as Christians talk about the Blood of Jesus Christ, we often refer back to the ole hymn "Nothing but the Blood," and in the chorus of the song it says "the blood will never lose its power." The blood of Jesus removes the stain of sin, makes you whole, gives you hope, peace and righteousness. It offers the promises of home, referring to Heaven. It reaches the highest mountains and the lowest valleys. It calms your fears and dries all of your tears. It gives you strength and ultimately gives you the power to overcome!

So again you ask, why did I start the book off this way? I did so to encourage each reader who may be experiencing what has been written so far, and for those who may experience what is yet to be read that you too can overcome. See, sin tries to beset you, but the blood delivers you. Life will sometimes break you, but the blood offers you wholeness. Experiences sometimes damage our hope, but the blood restores it.

The adversary tries to convince us there is nothing right about us, but the blood offers righteousness. You get the picture, right? There is redemptive, overcoming power in the blood of Jesus Christ. The blood of Jesus Christ is representative of the "Blood Covenant" and there is no stronger covenant than that of the Blood Covenant; the redemption of all mankind. *"And as they were eating, Jesus took bread, and blessed it, and brake it, and gave it to the disciples, and said, Take, eat; this is my body. And he took the cup, and gave thanks, and gave it to them, saying, Drink ye all of it; for this is my blood of the new testament, which is shed for many for the remission of sins"* (Matt. 26:26–28).

Can You Look Back Over Your Life and See?

Can you look back over your life and see areas where the blood of Jesus did more than provide salvation for you? Where the power of the blood of Jesus Christ was at work in your life? Have you ever considered where you would be if Jesus had not shed his blood for you? Had he not ascended to the Father, leaving us the precious Holy Spirit? Can you recall where the blood dried your tears and calmed your fears? How about offered you comfort and assurance? Have we relegated the very power of the blood of Jesus Christ to an ole song sung during communion? Is that what we have done with the precious blood of our Lord and Savior, Jesus Christ?

For me, the blood will never ever lose its wonder working power. I am able to write this book with encouragement, fire, joy and a zeal like never before because of the blood of Jesus Christ. I have openly shared what I have in this book, to first encourage you to never lose sight of the powerful working of the blood of Jesus Christ. To never, ever forget what it means! Secondly, to always remember its redeeming power, its restoration power, its wonder working power and its hope filled power. And lastly, there is life changing power in the Name and Blood of Jesus Christ. I will share with you how I know. Keep reading.

Each Story Is Relevant

On June 27, 2015, our nonprofit organization Sister's Celebrating Each Other, Inc. held our second annual women's conference. The theme was based on this very book, so we called it the *"2015 I Have Overcome Women's Conference."* We invited women speakers who had overcome everything from sexual assault, divorce, fear, domestic violence, cancer, incarceration to barrenness. As I sat and listened to the stories of each woman, I thought to myself, there is no way I need to be writing a book. These ladies have "real" stories to tell. I was amazed at the strength, perseverance, determination and resilience I had the honor of being in the same room with.

Later that evening as I drove home exhausted from what was a very long and tiring day, I pondered the day's events, stories, tears, laughter, fellowship and of course my book. I questioned whether, or not I had something book worthy to share. The next day the answer in my spirit was a resounding yes, you do. In fact, we all have a story to share and each one is not only relevant, but necessary.

Each story may not be put in print, bound and sold on the bookshelves, but rather conveyed through a series of greeting cards, poetically shared at the mic, or put to music in a beautiful song. They can be dramatically portrayed in plays, movies, and TV shows, or powerfully spoken at conferences and seminars. If shared, the effects are still to be life changing! The story is your testimony and the vehicle in which it is shared is irrelevant, so long as it's shared. The Word of God says in Revelations 12:11, *"And they overcame him by the blood of the Lamb, and by the word of their testimony; and they loved not their lives unto the death."* There is liberty in sharing your story, your testimony; not only for you, but for those who have an ear to hear the sound of freedom bells ringing through the testimony of another.

As we begin to take this journey together, I want you the reader to understand my heart, the purpose in which I believe I was charged by God to write this book. I believe God desires each of us to grab a hold to the experiences shared in this book, experiences we can relate to and touch us in very specific ways. Experiences that will provoke us to ponder and to search out the hidden things of the heart. Those experiences that caused us, or is currently causing us pain. Experiences we have perhaps refused to address, or don't know how to address, or we're too afraid to address. This book is designed and written to help many find liberty from those varying experiences that have had us bound, for far too long.

As we journey through the remaining chapters together and I unfold the many layers to my life's journey thus far, I do so with a desire to offer hope, encouragement and insight. My prayer is that each reader finds the courage and strength to reevaluate their lives and to seek God for needed change. Dare to revisit your life experiences and circumstances to see what wisdom and knowledge was being given through each one. Challenge your current belief systems with a goal to gain greater wisdom and to examine one's faith. To encounter a deeper and more intimate relationship with our God to whom there is so much more depth. The Word of God tells us in Romans 8:28, *"And we know that all things work together for good to them that love God, to them who are the called according to his purpose."* We may not always understand the reason or the methodology behind our experiences, but by this verse we should come to understand, despite the many challenges and difficulties in our lives, the end result is always to our benefit.

Now, before I close chapter one, I want each reader to know what the goals of the book are. I believe God gave me this book to offer to each reader encouragement, inspiration and motivation through sharing the triumphs and victory God alone has given to me. This book is to also offer hope and to help the reader to see the obstacles in their lives as opportunities, opportunities for overcoming. To see the power of God alive and active in their lives, despite what it may currently look like, or has looked like. I would like the reader to view and utilize this book as a workbook and not one you read once and set down. Now, before we move on to chapter two—stop right here. Grab a note book, a pen or pencil, an eraser, colored tabs, post-it notes, index cards, and a few highlighters. I firmly believe that if we want a specific thing, we must prepare to acquire it, and that takes preparation. Therefore, if you want to change you have to prepare for change. Case in point, if you're moving to a new location, you prepare to move with boxes, tape, bubble wrap, newspaper, movers, and a truck, right? Well, this book will help you move out from where you are and to inspire you to reach towards God to attain the fullness of life he desires for you. If God has brought me to the promises of my life, despite the journey of pain, darkness, barrenness, brokenness, loss and more. Let me encourage you that He will do it for you too! Remember the word of God in Deuteronomy 31:6 *"Be strong and of a good courage, fear not, nor be afraid of* *them: for the L*ORD *thy God, he it is that doth go with thee; he will not fail thee, nor forsake thee."*

As we move on, I also want you to be prepared to examine yourself through each page. At the end of some chapters, I have provided resources (links to websites) and references to articles I believe and hope will offer some insight. I have written prayers for your encouragement and utilization, and a series of questions I hope will encourage you. Don't feel as though you have to rush through each question, but rather take the time to meditate on the questions and ask God to help you find the truth in each one. Answer each question honestly and remember, the truth makes us free. Allow yourself to feel complete before moving on to the next chapter. There is no rush!

This book is meant for you to take your time and acquire what God is giving to you. He gave this book with each of you in mind. Receive what is being given. You should be experiencing encouragement, inspiration, motivation and growth with each chapter. At the end of each chapter, my hope is for you to see each obstacle you have or may face, as an opportunity for growth on all levels. Now, let's recap what you will need before we move on.

☐ Notebook or pad

☐ Pen and pencils

☐ Colored tabs

☐ Index cards

☐ Post-its

☐ Highlighters

If you checked yes to all of the above, then let's start chapter two.

Chapter Two

The Purpose, the Plan, the Process and the Plot

"And they overcame him by the blood of the Lamb, and by the word of their testimony; and they loved not their lives unto the death"

Rev. 12:11

These Are the Words I Heard

n 2002, I was sweeping my hallway getting prepared to wax my hardwood floors, which I loved to do. As I bent down to pick up the dust, I heard these words, *"Transparency is the bridge that builds trust."* I didn't know what the words meant, or what I was expected to do with them. This was not the first time I had heard words like this, words I knew were coming from God. I can recall another such experience when I heard words I knew were coming directly from God. This experience happened one afternoon walking home from the Bart station. I heard these words, *"If I take all their worldly possessions they have nothing, but to you I give my Spirit."* In each of these experiences, I may have had questions as to the experience itself, but there was absolutely no doubt as to who was doing the talking. My spirit knew the words were coming from God and God alone!

To this day I am not sure why, but this particular experience, where these particular words were being spoken, *"If I take all their worldly possessions they have nothing, but to you I give my Spirit,"* scared me. Maybe it was the depth of what was being said. Perhaps it doesn't sound that deep to read it now, but then it seemed the words spoke of a foretelling. As if God was preparing, or warning me of what was to come of my life. The words were future tense you know; speaking of things to come without saying what those things were. We know the Holy Spirit is the one through whom all the work is performed, so this meant work was about to be done and there was nothing that I could do about what was about to take place. Now we know the scripture says in Isaiah 55:11, *"So shall my word be that goeth forth out of my mouth: it shall not return unto me void, but it shall accomplish that which I please, and it shall prosper in the thing whereto I sent it."* To me, this indicated God was doing something, or had already done something in my life that was far beyond my understanding. It simply had not manifested yet and this scared me a lot!

There were two more occurrences in which I heard words spoken to me by God, including, *"Acknowledging what you don't have, places you in a position to receive what you need"* and *"It's not sleep you need, it's my Spirit."* I recall hearing the latter of the two when I was driving home early one morning and I was complaining about being tired and I cried out to God saying to him I needed more sleep. After he responded saying *"It's not sleep you need, it's my Spirit"* and the authority in which the words came, I hurried up and dried the tears from my eyes. This particular experience shook me to my core.

God speaks to us in many forms such as through his word, through prayer, through a song, through a pastor in the pulpit, or he speaks to us through a prophecy. When he speaks he does so with a specific goal. There is always a purpose (a reason), always a plan (a decision made of what will take place and how), there will always be a process (a series of actions to achieve the particular end) and there will always be a plot (many attempts to steal, kill and destroy God's purpose for your life). Let's look at Genesis. What was the purpose; the reason God spoke in the first place? It was to create, right? Okay, so now what was the plan? The plan was to take seven days to create everything that would be created. So now we begin the process, which is a series of actions to achieve the desired end. And then, finally the plot, we all know what happened to Adam and Eve, which was to steal, kill and to destroy God's ultimate plan for his creation.

Those series of actions began with God first speaking and creating heaven and earth, then he created the light, then he divided the light from the darkness and so on. You get the idea, right? There was a purpose, a plan and a process involved in what we see today. There was also a plot, the deception in the garden as noted above. When God spoke to me on the aforementioned occasions, it was with a purpose and a plan and there was certainly a process that would take place. Unfortunately, there would also be a plot to thwart the very plans of God in my life. A plot that would start long before my parents would even be aware of it.

I Now Know Who I Am in God

What was the purpose for my life, my birth, the very reason God spoke me into existence, called me by name, and placed me in my mother's womb to come forth to specific parents, at a specific era in time, and in a specific place? Would I ever know the purpose, the plan, or the process? Would I, or could I have imagined what all of this meant. If so, how long it would take for me to discover, or figure it out? What would it require? What would it cost? Where would all of this lead me as a result? How about the plot? Would I be made aware of the plot? What would it require for me to gain knowledge of such information? Today, I have an understanding and the answers to all of these questions. I know the purpose, because I now know who I am in God. I now see why the plan would take a period of time and the process would take a series of actions no one could have imagined, or anticipated would lead me to where I am today. I am also able to recognize the many plots by the adversary attempting to throw me off course. Trust me, there were some very good attempts made and had it not been for the blood, I would have succumbed to all of them. I am so grateful to God for his divine purpose, plan and his strategic process that rendered the plot of the enemy powerless in my life!

When God calls you it does not mean you will not have obstacles to overcome, it means you will come to understand you have already overcome, but you will have to endure the process. A process in which he tells you to *"Be strong and of a good courage, fear not, nor be afraid of them: for the* LORD *thy God, he it is that doth go with thee; he will not fail thee, nor forsake thee"* (Deut. 31:6). It means at the end of each phase of life, you learn to appreciate the process you endured to behold the promise. It means you learn to respect and reverence the cross in which your savior hung and the blood that flowed from his body, the sacrifice the Father made in love for you. It means you come to realize the gift your life is, the purpose for the talents and abilities you possess and the responsibility you've been given by virtue of being here. It means you come to understand there is a task at hand and that there is opposition on every side, but again, you come to both learn and understand you have already overcome, you are already victorious, triumphant, and you have already won!

I am only here today, writing a book on overcoming, because I have come to understand all of the above. Without enduring the process, there is no victory in overcoming the plot! This understanding has brought to fruition the truth of who I am today. I am a published author, the founder and executive director Sister's Celebrating

Each Other, Inc., a nonprofit organization. I am also the owner of A Gift of Love, a unique gift basket business and of CJA Enterprise. I am a business consultant, encourager, public speaker, and a licensed minister. All of these things did not come without growing pains.

Never settle for less than who you are and who you were created to be, regardless of the obstacles and how they may be disguised. Don't be shocked at what you face when you step into your purpose with God. You will begin to see and experience things that will look as though they are going to crush the very life out of you. You will feel like you are dying and you can't go any further, but stand firm in God. I am not going to kid you, pursuing purpose will be HARD and doing so will HURT, and you will want to escape from all of the pain. In these difficult times, always remember, if God be for you, who can be against you? I know, it's easier said than done, but all things are possible through Christ Jesus who strengthens us all. Never let the lie of what appears to be truth in your life, become the obstacles used to beset you. They're designed to obscure your vision and distort your perception. Instead, press onward and grasp every opportunity to live the life you were predestinated to live; a more abundant life, which you were promised. The life and all of the promises of God. They're all there, just on the other side of the varying challenges. Keep pushing!

All of these things I would have never-ever imagined myself being, or doing. But God had a purpose, a plan and set the course for a series of actions to bring me where I am today, long before I was born. We are his workmanship, created in Christ Jesus for good works and these good works were prepared beforehand according to Ephesians 2:10 *"For we are his workmanship, created in Christ Jesus unto good works, which God hath before ordained that we should walk in them."* God is the same yesterday, today, and forever. He will do the same for you, despite what it may look like, feel like, or it has been like. God is faithful to his word and his word declares, *"God is not a man that he should lie; neither the son of man that he should repent: hath he said, and shall he not do it? Or hath he spoken, and shall he not make it good"* (Num. 23:19).

Be Encouraged, God Is at Work

Your current situation has everything to do with your predetermined destination. In other words, nothing, no experience, be it good, bad or indifferent is ever lost with God. Regardless of the decisions, or the mistakes made to bring you to where you currently are. Even if where you find yourself was at the doing of someone else. God is bigger than every decision and every mistake any one of us has ever made, or will make, and of every wrong done to us. The cross validates this statement. Be encouraged; God is at work in the lives of his children and no devil in hell, including those invited in by disobedience, has the power to preempt God's divine, preordained plan and purpose for our lives. The only way this can change is if we choose to surrender our lives and power to the adversary and disobey God! God offers us the choice to choose life over death. Remember, when we as children of God, surrender to him and desire his will over our own, this is one of the many promises available to us in this life.

Now that we understand a little bit about the purpose, the plan, the process, and the plot, let's journey back into my childhood and see what all of this looked like in action in my life. Let me warn you, it's not a pretty picture, but it was all purposeful and God has and will continue to glorify himself in and through it all. Let's go.

My Journey

Over the years, I have spoken to many women and my story of overcoming is not very different from theirs. I'm sure it's not very different from your story either. Like so many others, I have overcome a spirit of fear, being homeless, sexual assault, physical abuse, suicidal thoughts, the loss of both parents, the inability to become a parent, the loss of possessions, the pain of divorce, the devastation of infidelity and more. But by the grace of God, I am still here today, to testify of God's faithfulness and his goodness towards his children.

My journey began when I was a child. I spent most of my childhood with my grandmother, lovingly known as "Big Mama" and now that I am grown I call her "Granny Granny." I loved spending time at my grandmother's house. It was fun and I got to spend time with my two aunts, Bay and Teresa, who still lived at home. My mother and her sisters were very close; it was the way my grandmother raised them. We never lived more than a block away from each other. Well, my mother was the one to move the furthest away, but my aunts stayed close to Big Mama.

I admired the female role models in my life; they were smart and beautiful both inside and out, and I wanted to be just like them when I grew up. My aunt Bay would pray with me every night before I went to bed. My aunt Teresa would take me shopping with her and teach me all about fashion. On our shopping adventures we would sing songs together and one such song was "One Less Bell to Answer" by the 5th Dimension. Man, we would sing that song as loud as we could and you should have heard me, I thought I was doing something.

One of the other things I loved about being at my grandmother's house was spending time with her in the kitchen. She would pull a chair up to the kitchen sink and teach me how to properly wash dishes . . . yes, at five-years old she was teaching me how to not only wash dishes, but how to cook and she cooked everything from scratch. I absolutely loved being at her house. My grandmother was always a very caring person and she still is. She would take care of a few neighbors on the block, going over to clean their houses and cook for those who were physically not able to do the chores themselves. She was always caring for someone else; helping in any way she could. I learned from watching her how to be selfless and how to care for others. Growing up, she would always talk to me about the bible and tell me stories about her father who was a minister.

She would, and still to this day, tells me stories of how he would attend great big tent meetings in and around Texas. She said people from all over would request and send for him to come and pray for them and how after he prayed, the sick would be healed. Out of all the times I spent with her and there are so many wonderful memories, it's our conversations about trusting in God I think of the most. Maybe it has something to do with me now being grown and having my own relationship with God. Perhaps, I can relate more now. I was with her when I first experienced someone being touched, or "filled" by the Holy Spirit. As a child, this scared the living daylights out of me (lol).

Although most of my childhood was spent living with my grandmother, the times I did spend with my mother were not all bad. Most of the time I spent with my mother, she was in a long-term relationship with someone she met when she was pregnant with me. In the times I recall being with them, I was taken care of. She taught me how to cook and clean. She was a neat freak, too, and would make sure our house was not only clean, but conduct full body inspections of me and my sister to make sure each bath we took produced clean bodies. I can recall having some happy times while she was in this relationship.

Every child loves their grandparents, and my stepfather's mother, sisters, and brothers, were all so very nice to us. I specifically have pleasant memories of spending time with his mother. As I write this passage, I can see her smiling face, her pigeon toes walking on the backs of her house shoes and if recalling correctly, she would wear this apron around her dress. I remember her bedroom was to the right as you walked in the front door of one of the places she lived. When we would go over to visit her, I would go straight to her room. As a child, it's good to hold pleasant memories and this is one such pleasant memory. As I am writing, I am recalling many more times with her, but I won't write about them all. Just know, they were very pleasant and have left a warm and fuzzy feeling in my heart. Whether we believe it or not, we do leave imprints on the lives of others and she has certainly left one on my life.

When It All Changed

I remember things changing for me when I was in elementary school. My mother's long-term relationship was on the brink of ending after a few years of relational issues, including a string of incidents of unfaithfulness in the relationship. I recall many arguments and fights. In one such fight, the fathers of my sister and brother were engaged in a gun fight against one another. Ducking behind the trees and telephone poles, one held me in front of him as they fired gun shots at each other. As a result, we had to move from the house we were living in at the time. For a period of time we lived with the family of my sister's father, and then over a period of time we would live with various other people; some friends and associates of my mother. My mother would eventually get another place of her own, but it was a far cry from the house we previously lived in. From what I can recall, my mother's long-term relationship was probably off and on for an extended period of time, maybe another four or five years before eventually ending all together.

As a result of her relationship ending, I watched my mother go through so much including increased drinking. This is a journey I would take with her. When I was around ten years old, we returned to LA and stayed a short while with my grandmother. It was during this time my mother gave birth to my second little brother.

After a while we would move back to San Bernardino, and in with some friends of my mothers. My mother's drinking continued to increase and her drinking buddies would sit around all day long, drinking from sun up to sun down. Eventually, my mother would lose both of her sons to their fathers.

The trauma of the relationship ending, only sent my mother spiraling more out of control and the drinking became even heavier. My mother's bout with alcoholism led to some unhealthy relationships and some of physical and verbal abuse. During this time, I formed a relationship with a young girl, one of my classmates, and we became best friends. It was pretty amazing. She was the youngest of her siblings and had recently lost her mother. It seemed like I was the only friend her dad would allow to come to her house. As I look back, we both really needed each other. She was the only one who seemed to relate to what I was going through and I was the only one who could relate to what she was going through. We were so close, that she would call my mother "mama." I, on the other hand, was terrified of her father and her siblings. I believe we were able to help each other through some very difficult times. Yes, even children need each other and relationships formed at a young age have more impact than most may realize. Our relationship to this day is evident of this fact.

The times we spent together are memories I will always cherish. Looking back, it was those times that got me through those difficult times. I was able to leave wherever we were living at the time, leave all the arguing, drinking and fighting and go to her house, be a kid and have fun times. I can remember on many occasions, standing outside of her front window, waiting for her dad to pull up in his brown Cadillac so I could go in. It was the only time living with my mother I can really recall being able to be my age! The times we had together were fun times. We would sing Prince songs together, making up dance steps and spending time sitting in her kitchen just doing silly kid stuff. We would spend time flipping and playing our made up games in her family room or hanging out in her bedroom. It didn't seem to matter what we were doing; our time together was soothing. I honestly believe it was these times that in their own way, nurtured us. Would you believe some thirty years later she would be my maid of honor at my second wedding? God is so amazing, right?

As a young girl, I watched the life of my mother, a beautiful young woman, dwindle away. I watched whatever self-esteem and self-worth she had die, leaving a shell. Over the course of the next two years, I would go back and forth living between my mother and my grandmother. However, it would not be long before I would return to live with my mother for a period of a year and yes, the drinking had gotten even worse if that's possible. I watched her endure so much physical abuse by the men in her life. She also endured the physical attacks of the significant others of these men, be it their wives or girlfriends and bearing witness to all of this became unbearable for me.

After a while, I simply could not take how we were living anymore. I was tired and in tears one night when I called my grandmother to come and get me. My heart hurt that night as I watched my mother sleeping off her early morning drinking session on the living room floor of someone's house we were staying with at the time. I can still recall the pain on my grandmother's face as we walked out the door and left my mother lying there on the floor. That night I cried all the way back to my grandparents' house in LA. I felt like I was my mother's protector and I was abandoning her. I was her only source of income (Welfare). What would she do without me? How would she live? What would she eat? Where would she stay? Who would protect her? These are all the questions I thought about as we drove back to LA. A child should never have to carry such a heavy burden and be faced with such adult decisions. I couldn't help but to wonder what my grandmother was thinking about leaving her oldest daughter lying there on the floor? Did she feel like a failure? Is there a certain number of attempts to helping your child before you decide it's enough? The dead silence in my grandfather's truck as we drove back to LA was in a word, LOUD.

I Had No Idea

A year later, I returned to live with my mother. I had no idea what the next three years would bring. The drinking at this point had consumed her. She was losing weight, her stomach was swelling due to the cirrhosis of the liver and she was involved in another unhealthy relationship. She suffered more physical assaults from those who would wait until they found her drunk to assault her. I helped so many times to cover her black-eyes and busted lips with make-up. On occasion, I found myself defending her the best I could; engaging in bouts with her attackers. During this time, I had an aunt who did not live too far away and sometimes to get away from all of the craziness I would go to her house and she would allow me to stay a few days. Her house was a place of solitude and comfort for me. It felt like home; something I did not have with my mother.

My mother's continued drinking led to more bad decisions and choices, which only led to more devastation and heartache. How do I know? I was there and I witnessed it all! The painful memories of things I witnessed my mother experiencing such as physical abuse, being beaten with pipes in her face and to hear people who were supposed to be her friends talking about her was very hard for me and would be for any child.

On many different occasions I witnessed my grandmother trying to help my mother. Why was the help not effective? What happened to her? Was her pain rooted too deep? If so, is any pain too deep for God? What causes a beautiful young woman to self-destruct? Was it self-destruction, or was it simply God's love that took her home? If that's the case, then what about us, the children who were left with a massive void and immeasurable pain? I have had so many questions over the years. Especially now that I am a grown woman. Even after all these years, it's these questions that I still ponder on, asking why?

It was the last time I returned to live with my mother that I was sexually assaulted twice; once by a so-called "close family friend"—and by someone who was like a father to me. I asked myself who could I have told: my grandmother? Yes, I could have told her, but I did not want to cause my mother more pain and embarrassment. What child, after witnessing their parent go through so much pain, would want to add more? Even today, we see kids trying to sell drugs to lighten the financial burden and stress of their parents. This is something no child should have to take on or experience. Looking back, I often ponder why my mother's life was like it was? Why did she have to die so young? Why so much pain? Why did God allow it? Why was she not saved, or was she? Why God could not save her, or did he? Why, with a mother who was so spiritually-grounded, did she not go to her mother for help, or did she? Did she not want help? So many questions and all unanswered. Perhaps, it's best this way.

What Happened to Her

My mother was beautiful, smart and she was brought up well. My grandmother has told me over and over again my mother was a well-mannered child, but something happened to her when she was a teenager. What was it? What happened to her that changed her? Could it have stemmed from her childhood experiences? Could it have come from moving away from her natural father and Native American heritage? Could it have come from being adopted by her stepfather then being removed from this relationship too? Was it a result of developing young love and having it end painfully? Did it all start with her becoming pregnant at such a young age and enduring that alone? I often wonder, could her plot in life have begun when she was a child? Notice I said "PLOT"— the enemy's plot to thwart the plan of God in her life and possibly the lives of her children. Remember the purpose, the plan, the process, and the PLOT?

Now that I am a grown woman, my childhood experiences raise even more questions and concerns for me than before. These concerns include questions such as how many children today are experiencing sexual assault? How many are living with a parent, or parents who suffer with an addiction? How many are being abused, be it neglect, homelessness, or worst? What about those who feel called of God and do not understand what they are experiencing. How do any of them handle the fear of sharing what they are experiencing? Chances are, as a result of these experiences they are not seeking the help they may need? Is this why our young children, both girls and boys are turning to gangs to experience the bond of family and find a sense of security? How many young girls, teenagers, and young women are experiencing self-worth and self-esteem issues? Issues that have landed them in unhealthy relationships in search of finding acceptance and being drawn to a false sense of love. How many of them are intentionally trying to become pregnant to satisfy the void of their understanding of unconditional love? When does the vicious cycle end?

When pain is not identified and dealt with properly, it opens the doors to so much more than we care to imagine. How many times have those of us in the church often talked about seeds being planted? Now let me ask you this question: how often do we talk about the seeds the adversary plants in our lives? In the lives of our children? Would you dare consider such seeds are being planted early in your child's life? There are seeds of words being planted in our children's lives, long before we are suspecting of such a deadly attack.

The seeds are those of neglect, verbal abuse and dare I say more? I know, you don't curse your child, but in frustration are you calling them stupid, dumb, or worse? Are others calling into existence things into their lives you are not aware of? Have you called your daughter ugly, skinny, fat, or worse? Is someone else? These are all seeds, the seeds of words we and others are speaking and planting in our children's lives. These are the labels and titles we assign to our children by the very words spoken over and into their lives. Guess what, those seeds, they produce a harvest too. The process does not change because of where the seed or planting originates; it still produces either good fruit or bad fruit. What type of fruit are you bringing or allowing to be brought forth? Parents, we must pay attention to the cunning attacks of the adversary and be careful not to align ourselves by agreeing with his tactics and doing so unsuspectingly by what we say or allow others to say to and over our children. This is how he steals, kills, and destroys lives so cunningly and early in life. Please, be wise and pay attention!

My mother suffered from alcoholism, which is a spirit of bondage. Did anyone every stop to ask why? Where did this come from? What door was opened in her life that led to this? Why are we, as a people, so quick to judge without ever asking why? Without ever taking the time to go before God in earnest prayer and inquire to know his heart on the matter at hand. The word of God says in 2 Peter 3:9 *"The Lord is not slack concerning his promise, as some men count slackness; but is longsuffering to us-ward, not willing that any should perish, but that all should come to repentance."*

In short, this means he will exhibit patience with us because he would rather we ALL come to repentance to partake of his promises. So why don't we exhibit such patience with our loved ones? Are they not worth it? Is there a time to quit and relinquish hope? What would our Savior do? He would go to the cross that we might have an opportunity at life and life more abundantly.

Are we ready to make such hefty sacrifices for our loved ones? I find it amazing that we all want mercy from God through Jesus Christ, but we are unwilling to give mercy to others. We don't want to be judged, but we so quickly judge others. We don't want anyone talking and gossiping about us, but we have no quarrels about talking and gossiping about others—and we call ourselves Christians. Can I get an Amen!

So we can see by where God has brought me, there was clearly a purpose, right? We've seen a little bit of both the plan and of the process, but what we've seen most in this chapter, is of the plot. Not only in my mother's life, but possibly in my life. The enemy starts as I've mentioned multiple times early on in the lives of our children. The seeds that were planted in my life did not only come by words I heard, but by what I saw and experienced. The gun battle was supposed to kill me, but God. The pain and devastation of what I saw my mother go through was supposed to cause me to turn to a different lifestyle, but God. The rape and molestation, they were supposed to break me in every possible way, but God. The embarrassment of it all was supposed to wreck the dream and purpose God sent me here with, but God. I was supposed to be a heavy drinker, strung out on drugs, and given to a promiscuous life, but God!

There is still time to reverse the curse in the lives of your children and your loved ones. You can speak life over them. You can decree the word of God over their lives. You can seek God in fasting and in prayer on their behalves; asking him who they are and what is their destiny? Please, don't leave the lives of your children, or your loved ones to chance? Are they not worth it? Do you not desire for them to live a life of purpose? Do you want them to live the very life God predestinated them to live? Don't just hand them over to the enemy so easily and without a fight. Is that the way you would treat such a precious gift from God? Each of our lives are precious to God, so much so that according to John 3:16 *"For God so loved the world, that he gave his only begotten Son, that whosoever believeth in him should not perish, but have everlasting life."* If our lives are that precious to him, then how much more shall they be to us?

Your children are gifts from God. Gifts he has entrusted you to usher into their divine purposes. Honor him with the lives of your children. Be GREAT stewards over them. There is still time; it's not too late. Beseech the father and redirect their course in life. Their age does not matter. It really doesn't so long as they still have breath, there is hope!

Key Points:

As you read through "The Purpose, the Plan, the Process and the Plot," can you:

- Look back over your life and recall moments where God clearly spoke to you? If so, be it through a sermon at church, reading the bible or sitting during a quiet hour. Those moments are priceless. Journal them as you experience them, if you have not been doing so. It will help serve as a huge source of encouragement for you!

- Can you see where life experiences may have been meant for bad, and how God has turned them all around for good in your life? If so, examine those moments and I guarantee you, you will have a different outlook on your life and the course it has taken.

- Looking over your life thus far, can you see the strategy in which God has ordered your steps, regardless of what it may have looked like? Okay, shall we have a praise break right here?

- Has this chapter opened your eyes to see your life, your children's lives, and the lives of your loved ones differently? If so, how?

- Do you feel empowered? Empowered to pray for your children and loved ones? Empowered to work with God and see your loved ones living their divinely predestined lives? If so, GREAT!

If you are currently on your journey and cannot answer these questions at this time, it's all right. They are designed to provoke you to inquire, seek out, and ask of God. The story, the journey, and the process may be different, but the God who has given you the power to overcome is the same! As you read my story and journey from chapter to chapter, I pray you find encouragement, inspiration, and motivation to overcome.

Prayer:

Beloved and merciful Father, I pray right now as I hold this book in my hands with many questions, concerns, fears and yes, even some doubts as to how I am going to continue. I ask you to strengthen me right now, Lord God. Father, I am in a situation and I cannot see my way out of this situation. Please remind me that you are my strong tower, my present help in times of trouble. Remind me that you are the great I AM and that I am the apple of your eye. Remind me of your everlasting mercy and kindness towards me shown in and through Jesus Christ. Remind me Father that you will never leave nor forsake me, according to your word. Allow me to feel the warmth of your loving arms around me and remind me you will bestow upon me a crown of beauty instead of ashes, the oil of joy instead of mourning, and a garment of praise instead of a spirit of despair. Remind me that I will be called an oak of righteousness, a planting of the LORD for the display of his splendor. Give me the confidence to know that I am fearfully and wonderfully made; that your works are wonderful. May I know full well, all these things and sing your praises in Jesus' Name I pray, Amen!

Father, I am a mother who holds my children and my loved ones up to you right now with a renewed hope in the redemptive Blood and Love of my Lord and Savior Jesus Christ and I thank you, Lord God for such a hope. Father, I stand encouraged in your word that my children and my loved ones are each words, spoken out of the mouth of God, words that will not return unto you void, but instead words that will go forth and accomplish that which pleases you. Help me to be anchored in your word and in the fact that you are not a man that you should lie, nor are you the son of man that you should repent. Help me to realize that you are God and if you spoke it, you will perform it! Help me to stand firmly upon your word that states neither death, nor life, nor angels, nor principalities, nor things present, nor things to come, nor powers, nor height, nor depth, nor any other created thing will be able to separate me, my children or my loved ones from the love of God, which is in Christ Jesus. Help me not to condemn, judge, or tear my children or my loved ones down in frustration or anger with my words using my small, but very powerful and dangerous tongue. For my children and loved ones who know no better than to believe they are enslaved to sin, encourage their hearts today, Father. Bring them to a place of prayer, where they can come to know and seek you for their deliverance and the subsequent abundant life you promised us. Continue to show me what it means to love without limits as I seek you daily for the light to be revealed to my children and my loved ones. Continually show me what is means when you said "love covers a multitude of sin." Continually show me how to stand firmly rooted and planted in love, holding tight that none of my children or my loved ones should perish, but that all would come to repentance and know the saving grace of our Lord and Savior Jesus Christ. Father God, let me no longer be a person of talk, but of action. Help me become a committed and diligent doer of the word of God and not just a mere hearer of the Word. Show forth your glory Father, and let me rejoice in not only my children and loved ones returning to a relationship with you the Father, but all mankind as my prayers are not of a selfish nature! I will be forever careful to give you all the praise and all the glory as I watch in great expectation and anticipation to see all of your children calling out to you, Abba my Father. I pray this prayer in Jesus' Holy Name, Amen!

Chapter Three

Reflection and the Difference Three Years Make

"To everything there is a season, and a time to every

purpose under the heaven..."

Ecclesiastes 3:1

What Happened to Her Mother?

I know, you have a ton of questions running through your minds; questions like what happened to her mother? How did she die? When did she die? What led her down this path and how does this all tie in with overcoming? Well, in order to go forward, I am going to have to go backwards first.

My mother found herself pregnant at the age of sixteen. She tried to conceal her pregnancy by imitating her girly monthly very creatively, but her creative genius was short-lived. My grandmother soon found out she was pregnant and from what I was told, she was not very happy with the situation.

Although unhappy with my mother's current situation, my grandmother was a very supportive mother and she would be a strong sense of support for her oldest daughter. After coming to terms with the situation at hand, my grandmother and my uncle Leonard reportedly escorted my mother over to my father's house. I was told when confronted with my mother's pregnancy, the boy with whom my mother was so enamored with denied my mother was carrying his child. I was also told this was a very painful time for my mother, even at sixteen-years old.

SIDE BAR: *To my father's defense, he would later tell me their relationship had ended and she was dating someone else, so he thought the other gentlemen was my father. It was never my father's desire to deny me . . . we'll talk more about my daddy, who I loved dearly later.*

My grandmother did not believe in abortion, so my mother would continue in her pregnancy and before I was born, my grandmother relocated to a new city. Perhaps this all had something to do with my mother becoming pregnant and my father (at the time) denying the pregnancy. Maybe it was my grandmother's way of protecting her daughter and giving her a fresh start. To these questions, we will never know the answer. These are all my assumptions and nothing more.

With relocating, excitement soon revealed itself in great anticipation and expectation of my arrival. I can still recall my aunts telling me the story of my first day home from the hospital and how excited they were. Home from school, they came screaming and shouting "where's the baby, where's the baby" and in the midst of their bliss as new celebrated aunties they actually tossed their school books right on top of me! I can recall so many wonderful stories of happy moments; moments of laughter that birthed such great memories. Unfortunately, they would be covered up by the many more painful experiences that would soon darken my mother's life.

You see, my mother's pain could have very well started when my grandmother and her natural father separated and she had to leave the early life she knew on the Indian reservation in Oklahoma. They left Oklahoma for Arizona, where my grandmother met and married granddaddy Johnson, and together they bore my two aunts, Teresa and Frances (Bay), and he adopted my mother. When this relationship ended my grandmother then relocated back to California and the relationship with my mother and father resulted in me.

When their relationship ended, my grandmother relocated. Living in a new city and attending a new school, my mother met and began dating her high school sweetheart. From what I understand the relationship started off as a healthy one, but became a tumultuous one that would last well over ten years. During this time, my mother would give birth to my sister, outside of the relationship. A few years later, the two of them would have a son; my mother's first boy. A couple of years after that, she would give birth to her fourth and final child, my baby brother from another relationship.

In identifying the onset of my mother's pain I did some research on the effects of separation and how and what those affects are in children, and in their adult life. This article from the North Carolina Division of Social Services and the Family and Children *Resource Programs is rather old, but offers some good information. In this article, they* suggest, *"Separating a parent and child can also have profoundly negative effects. Even when it is necessary, research indicates that removing children from their homes interferes with their development. The more traumatic the separation, the more likely there will be significant negative developmental consequences. Repeated separations interfere with the development of healthy attachments and a child's ability and willingness to enter into intimate relationships in the future. Children who have suffered traumatic separations from their parents may also display low self-esteem, a general distrust of others, mood disorders (including depression and anxiety), socio-moral immaturity, and inadequate social skills.* Shared from the Jordan Institute for Families. You can read more on this article on their website via the below link: http://www.practicenotes.org/vol2_no4/effects_of_separation_and_attachment.htm.

In another article by the **"Australian Government Initiative"** I found this information very informative under the topic "How do they behave" *"Children do not always communicate with words. Their responses to their parents' separation may be expressed in behavior. Some children become very **withdrawn** and avoid talking about the separation or the absent parent. Others (particularly if they are younger) may become very 'clingy' and not want to let the parent they are with out of their sight. These children feel they have 'lost' the departing parent and are determined not to lose their remaining parent."* You can find this article and more on children and separation at their website at the following link: *http://www.*

familyrelationships.gov.au/BrochuresandPublications/
Pages/ChildrenAndSeparationBooklet.aspx.

In Retrospect

In discussions I've had with my grandmother, aunts, and my father, I found out that my mother was considered a shy young lady up until her high school years. Looking back, I wonder if the term *"shy"* accurately articulated who she was, or what she was experiencing. Was she withdrawn from the many degrees of separation she endured? Did each separation she experience contribute to her demonstrating low self-esteem and low self-worth, preventing her from developing healthy attachments, or relationships later in life? My guess would be quite possibly, yes.

Often times we don't ask why a child may be acting out. We just as easily assume the child needs to be disciplined. If the child is quiet, we assume they're shy. If the child is acting a certain type of way, we may cast it off by saying things like "that's just the way they are ."

Yeah, but my question is still why? Why are they acting that way? We can safely surmise from my mother's life this fact for sure "if we easily overlook the effects of separation, it can and will trigger the onset of a list of life-long problems if not properly handled." We can also safely surmise how issues not properly identified and addressed can have a devastating effect on a person's entire life and in the lives of their children. Hence, the story of my mother and her children.

From a natural and spiritual standpoint, we must pay close attention and not ignore the warning signs in our children. We must then delicately and diligently explore the origin and take the necessary steps to achieving overall wholeness in the lives of our children. We've already noted when pain is not identified and properly dealt with, we can open the doors to issues such as alcoholism, drug addictions, promiscuity and more into our lives, and the lives of our children.

SIDE BAR: *Imagine if you will for a moment, being a young girl twice removed from the father figures in her* *life, finding herself in a puppy-love relationship and we all know how real these relationships can be to a young girl and then add to that, having your first child denied. My father's denial (at the time) could have meant to her he denied everything she thought they had. This heartbreak alone translates into the mind of a sixteen-year-old girl as "rejection" the same rejection she experienced via the separation from her father and stepfather. Even though they did not reject her, these feelings were birthed possibly, through each experience of separation.*

See how quite possibly the adversary starts early on in his plan to steal, kill and destroy. He starts long before most of us are even aware of it. We're busy having baby showers, celebrating our children's birthday's and other events without ever really giving any thought to the assignments out on our children, or our loved ones for that matter. Most of these attacks begin before our children can even talk. Can I remind you of King Herod in the bible? When he learned the King and the Savior was being born, he ordered every male child under two years old to be killed in an effort to stop God's plan in Jesus' life from coming to pass. As if he had any power to do that! Yet, he still carried out his objective. There is no difference in the lives of our children today, the attacks are still very imminent! The only difference is those in biblical days strictly adhered to what God instructed them to do. Today, are we even considering the possible attacks on the lives of our children and loved ones? Not only that, but is it quite possible that we're too busy with life to even notice the looming attacks? I've had instances where loved ones landed in jail, in the hospital or other things happened and I asked the question of God "was I spiritually asleep, too busy to be in tune with you spiritually to pray or possibly fast? Have you asked the question of God? Would we even obey God's instruction if we did or were in tune and aware? We all have purposes; every one of God's creation does and they're worth fighting for. Although the method in which the adversary is trying to steal the purpose, kill the life and destroy the plan has changed from those of biblical days, please hear me, the threat and objective is still very real today! Please spend time with God in prayer for your children and loved ones! It's imperative that we do!

SIDE BAR: *Mother's listen, the adversary launches an attack on your children long before they reach adulthood. His attacks begin with things like rejection, pain, neglect, etc. Do not be fooled, hoodwinked, and bamboozled any further by the tactics of the adversary. Do not be spiritually ignorant to his tactics.*

The enemy is after our purpose in life, which is the Will of God. Since the purpose of God is brought forth through us, the strategy begins very early in life, sometimes in the womb (hence my earlier statement) with our children. The enemy is cunning, sly and very strategic. Arm yourselves with wisdom from God. No longer allow the enemy to distract you with situations and circumstances presented by life to cause you to fail to pay close attention to your children and loved ones. Speak life over your children and loved ones. Declare the Word of God over them daily. If possible, pray for them and with them daily. Regarding your children, the word says in Proverbs 22:6 *"Train up a child in the way he should go: and when he is old, he will not depart from it."* We should live the lives we desire our children and loved ones to live by being a good example of wholesome living before them. All of us should not merely talk the talk, but we should be walking the walk. We should no longer get so bogged down with the busyness of life that we leave access points and open portals to our children and to our loved ones and families as a whole.

Now that we have done some much needed reflection on my mother's early life and the cunning attacks of the adversary on our children and our loved ones. Let's examine what the next three years of my life with my mother would bring. *"To everything there is a season, and a time to every purpose under the heaven"* (Ecclesiastes 3:1). Who would have thought that this time, when I returned to live with my mother it would be for the last time? Certainly not me. Who imagines their visit with a loved one or friend to be their last? Their last conversation to be their last? Their last kiss before a loved one leaves to be their last? None of us do, right?

What a Difference Time Makes

The last three years of my mother's life (from the age of thirty to thirty-three) would prove to be a pivotal time in my life (from the age of thirteen to sixteen). During this time, I can recall living at many different places and many people's houses (I wouldn't necessarily call them homes), not including the various motels we lived in. The many times we stayed in motels affected my ability to attend school on a regular basis. I missed so much school and transferred so many times that I fell behind in my course work.

Perhaps some of you can relate to missing so much school and not being there to hear instructions on assignments that you become embarrassed to return. By this time, you realize you have run out of excuses because you've used them all before. This was my story. Some of my classmates were aware of what was going on in my life and this made it even more embarrassing for me to go back to school. The sad thing is, I really loved to learn and I actually liked attending school.

Having the potential to graduate with good grades proved to be unattainable. I simply had far too many absences and I just could not pull it off. Even though I received good grades when I attended school, it wasn't enough, and I ended up having to go to a continuation school because of my failing grades. I didn't get the opportunity to finish school or walk the stage to receive my diploma and for a very long time I felt like I was robbed. I had high hopes of attending college when I graduated. Unfortunately for me, this was not how my school days' story would go.

SIDE BAR: *I've heard it said that children are resilient and while that "may" be true, I've also heard numerous stories of where children suffer in their adolescent, early adult and adult years from childhood experiences. We have to pay closer attention to our children. Perhaps then, we can gain an understanding of the effect and* *impact childhood experiences are having in the lives of our adults. Sometimes these results end in death, hence my mother's story.*

It was also during the last three years of my mother's life that she was diagnosed with what the doctor would described as a "touch" of cirrhosis of the liver. She was told specifically by the doctor if she stopped drinking, she would be okay. I accompanied her to this doctor's appointment and I can still recall being that fifteen-year old child sitting in that doctor's office with my mother and thinking I had to do something to save her life. I did not want my mother to die. What child does? That memory burns in my mind even today. I can still see the doctor's building across the street from the hospital where I was born. I can still see the room we sat in, the stool in which the doctor sat, the color of the building, the look on her face and the feeling in the pit of my stomach. It's all still very real to me. It's amazing what we stash deep inside and how we continue on as if these experiences never happened. Be careful, this can be a very unhealthy way of living.

I knew she was drinking and drinking heavily. I watched her and her friends every day do the same thing over and over again. She would wake up at six in the morning every day and make sure we (my sister and I, when my sister was with us) had what we needed for school. Her friends, (or rather her drinking partners) would show up like clockwork, just in time for the corner liquor store to open. The special knock on the door of whatever house or motel we were staying in at the time was always the same identifier.

They would gather their coins and dollar bills and then decide who was going to go to the store. Once they had their lot, they would sit all day drinking bottle, after bottle, after bottle of either Vodka, or Gin, whichever one they could afford that morning. It would not be long before the arguing and fighting would start and this was an everyday occurrence. In an effort to keep my mother healthy and prevent her from dying, I would hide their bottles or pour them out. She and her friends would get so mad at me. Especially after they had put their pennies together to buy the bottle, or bottles, that I had just hidden or poured out.

I would talk to her so-called friends, pleading with them to not offer her any alcohol or buy her anything to drink. I didn't understand that I was dealing with alcoholics and that alcoholism is a disease and a form of bondage, and most people cannot help themselves. I was pleading and begging people who had an addiction to help me. I was a child trying to deal with manipulative adults who were driven by their addiction. People who wanted nothing but to get their hands on another drink. They were not interested in trying to save mother's life. Needless to say, they were not taking into consideration any of my conversations, nor concerns regarding my mother's life. They only wanted to satisfy their desire to drink!

Why Do We Do What We Desire Not to Do

Growing up and watching someone you love so much, suffer from such a horrific addiction is heart-wrenching. To this day I hate drinking. Have I tried drinking before? Absolutely! As a teenager, my friends and I would drink. I never drank a lot because I hated both the taste and the smell of alcohol. But yep, I drank. Sure, I can tell you it was because of what was around me. I can tell you it was the atmosphere, that it was my norm. Why does a woman who is being beaten and abused stay with her abuser? Why does a person stay after being molested, or not tell anyone about being molested? I am no therapist, but I've learned from my own experiences that sometimes the explanation is unexplainable. I know to some this statement will make no sense whatsoever, but it's true. It's funny, looking back and knowing I hated the taste and the smell of alcohol, yet I still drank. I don't know why I did it.

Even now I sometimes think about why I did what I really didn't like doing? What was my point in doing so? Was I trying to fit in? Was I trying to be a part of the crowd? I got along good with my friends so there was no peer pressure. Besides, I was never one to follow. So why did I feel like I had to do what I really didn't want to do? Even after bearing witness first hand to the devastating effects of drinking and alcoholism through my mother? I drank as an adult, too and doing so reminded me of everything I experienced as a child with my mother and drinking with my friends. It wasn't long before I decided it was okay to be true to who I was. I no longer felt like I had to do what everyone else was doing. I finally resigned myself to the fact that it was okay to be Ceola and no longer drink—or smoke weed, for that matter. Yep, I did that too.

It's amazing how you can grow up experiencing things and even though everything in you is screaming "NO, this is not me and not what I want" and yet your environment is screaming "YES, this is your life, who you are, what you have, and yes, it's what you want." I thank God that was not my truth, nor is it your truth. I made the decision to agree with my inner man, my instinct, my spirit, the true me. I dared to believe I was different, not better, just different. I dared to believe that I could have different, that I could choose to have a different life and that it was okay to do so.

Because my mother was drinking heavily, I was a thirteen-year-old child cashing the welfare checks and paying debt we owed and I'm not talking about debt from household bills. More like her tab at the liquor store or money that was borrowed to buy alcohol when the tab at the liquor store was too high. I was grocery shopping with her food stamps and all of this led to me being teased often and made fun of by those who knew what was going on. Now, don't get me wrong, I was never afraid to stand up for myself and I have never been one to not speak my mind and back it up if necessary, but that did not make it all easier. Sometimes I think back and I know that God certainly had His hands upon me—how else could I have survived it all?

Your Victory Does Not Need to be Proven

The last three years of my mother's life indeed held some pretty painful memories I've tried to bury deep with a desire to never relive them again. I have refused to go back to where I experienced all of the pain due to the memories associated with it. To this day my siblings don't understand why I won't go and visit my mother's grave, or why I rarely go and visit them. I am indeed an overcomer, but that does not mean I desire to return to the place of my pain. I don't have to do that to be assured that I have overcome. I am already assured of my overcoming by the blood of my Savior alone. I have made a conscious choice not to return to the place of my pain and that's my choice to make. Unless, of course God sends me back.

I have no doubt that it was the grace of God and His mercy that I had a grandmother who loved the Lord and who was my shield. She was the one who kept me grounded and stopped what I am sure would have been a lot more heartache and dysfunction. There are blessings and curses in our generational bloodlines. Through prayer and fasting, we can break the generational curses and strongholds and God can and will redeem and restore the generational blessings that are also in our blood lines. Both are present, but we have to choose and follow the course of action obediently.

We must be willing to seek God's face; looking beyond what can be seen to inquire of what cannot be seen. We have to be willing to stand in the gap through earnest prayer and fasting. Willing to enter into war with a determination to be victorious! This type of battle is not for the faint at heart, but for those who are serious and who will not flinch at the adversaries over used tactics. We already have the victory, but it does not manifest without a fight. Are you fully prepared to go into battle, to take back the lives and purposes of our children, loved ones and friends? Are you ready to truly fight the good fight of faith?

In closing this chapter, I want to reiterate my purpose for sharing my mother's story was not in any way to cast a cloud over her life. But rather to draw attention to what can happen if we're not wise to the cunning attacks of the enemy and be willing to learn the spiritual strategy for rendering him powerless and reclaiming the purposes and the lives of our loved ones. Let me just clarify this; my mother was the best mother she knew how to be. While it appears most of the experiences I had with my mother rendered pain, we did have times where beautiful memories were birthed. My mother was a beautiful person inside and out. She was kind, and would give you the shirt off her back. I am using my childhood, the last three years of her life and my adult life, to prayerfully shed some much needed light and to offer hope. I pray the lives of women and children will be changed for the better after reading this book.

I pray that my mother's story would be used in honor of her memory, to act as a point of reference and a guiding light to many other women, young and mature alike, and to their children. I pray this book and the sharing of her story would add an extension to the purpose of her life in being a mother. That it would mean her life had a farther reaching impact and can change the lives of many for the better. My mother was born Devoria Swift, adopted and later called Devoria Johnson. She passed away on September 27, 1983 at the age of thirty-three. She was laid to rest ten days before my 17th birthday on October 8, 1983.

My father was also a great father to me and left me with wonderful experiences and memories. Both of my parents have left impacts on my life that I will forever cherish. I have learned a great deal from the both of them, and I am thankful for the time, however short it was, I was allowed to spend with them. As for my grandmother (granny granny), she has always been a wonderful source of encouragement to me. Even faced with the challenging onset of dementia, to this day as I write the pages to this book, she is my constant and faithful cheerleader. Always telling me to put my trust in God, faithfully declaring "He won't lead you wrong." She told me God was going to bless this book and I believe her.

My plea:

Please, don't look at a loved one who seems to be different, or in your opinion difficult and cast them off. Take the time to earnestly beseech God on their behalf. Remember, it is the will of the Father the NONE should perish according to 2 Peter 3:9 *"The Lord is not slack concerning his promise, as some men count slackness; but is longsuffering to us-ward, not willing that any should perish, but that all should come to repentance."*

I encourage you to learn to do as the Father does and that is to look beyond the faults of those who may be struggling, regardless of the area of struggle and see their need for deliverance. We must show them the way by speaking the truth and exposing them to the light. We simply cannot afford to leave not one. We must love as God has loved us. John 3:16 says this, *"For God so loved the world, that he gave his only begotten Son, that whosoever believeth in him should not perish, but have everlasting life."* We must also be determined and willing to do as Jesus shared in the parable of the lost sheep in Luke 15:1–7 *"Then drew near unto him all the pub-licans and sinners for to hear him. And the Pharisees and scribes murmured, saying, This man receiveth sin-ners, and eateth with them. And he spake this parable unto them, saying, what man of you, having an hundred sheep, if he lose one of them, doth not leave the ninety and nine in the wilderness, and go after that which is lost, until he find it? And when he hath found it, he layeth it on his shoulders, rejoicing. And when he cometh home, he calleth together his friends and neighbours, saying unto them, rejoice with me; for I have found my sheep which was lost. I say unto you, that likewise joy shall be in heaven over one sinner that repenteth, more than over ninety and nine just persons, which need no repentance."*

Key Points:

- To overcome is to succeed in dealing with a problem or difficulty. There are many who have overcome many trials in their lives. There are also those who are looking for something, anything, to help them overcome. I overcame a tumultuous child-hood that included rape, alcoholism, the death of my mother when I was sixteen years old, embarrassment and shame as a child, academic failure, and much more. The point is that I have overcome because the blood of Jesus will never, ever lose is power. We have got to get to the point where we truly believe God's word. I mean we must really take him at his word. His word is effective and it WILL bring about a change, but only when we dare to believe!

- Bad experiences don't have to remain bad; we can overturn evil with good according to the word of God in Romans 12:21 *"Be not overcome of evil, but overcome evil with good."* This very verse lets us know we will have experiences and if we yield "authority," over to them, they can overtake us. However, the second part tells us how to overturn evil with good. What is the "good" factor in your life? Well, Genesis tells us that as God created the earth and everything therein, he looked back upon his work and called it "good"—that includes us. Just as he created the earth with a purpose, so are we created and therefore, we should be doing what we were created to do, his purpose in and for our lives. That good and perfect will. In other words, do not focus on the evil, "fret not," but rather focus on God and his will for your lives. Therein is the power to overcome.

- We all have experiences in life and those experiences, depending on how we see them, can either make us stronger or they can break us and make us weak. I'm not saying our experiences don't hurt us, nor am I suggesting we can easily recover from them. What I am stating is that we can certainly overcome them and be victorious and better as a result. The game changer is in how we perceive them. Change your perception, change your outcome. This does not mean the experience or the journey will be different, it means your attitude while journeying through will be different and therefore, your result will be different.

- I understand this is not an overnight evolving; it's a process that will yield a great reward. Be encouraged. Overcoming is a choice that's made available to us and it's a journey that leads to victory!

Rape is one of the worst violations anyone, female or male can experience. Especially when it is committed by someone you trust and by someone who is supposed to protect you. Many times those who are raped will push this experience to the back of their minds and continue to live life as if nothing ever happened or as if nothing is wrong with them. One of the many potential reasons for this approach could be the result of guilt, as if they themselves did something to bring this action on. It can be shame and the fear of what people will think about them if they knew. It can be embarrassment with regard to how people will look at them as a result of knowing they've been raped. If not dealt with, people who have experienced sexual assault can experience issues with trust, depression, become suicidal, and so much more. If you or someone you know has experienced sexual assault or any of the above mentioned issues, please talk to someone, or call the National Sexual Assault Hotline at: 1–800–656-HOPE (4673) or you can visit their website at *https://rainn.org/*. You don't have to suffer alone. Please talk to someone and do so sooner rather than later. Rape and sexual assault is NEVER the fault of the person violated. It is a violent violation that no one deserves. Please, report it and take the power over your life back! You may have been victimized, but you are NOT THE VICTIM!

Alcoholism doesn't just affect the person who is drinking, it affects everyone in their circle; be it the spouse, the children, other family members, friends or associates. Alcoholism places the entire family and circle of loved ones at risk. If you, someone you know or someone in your family is facing alcoholism and efforts to get the person to attend a program or counseling are failing; please know there are programs for friends and family members of alcoholics to attend. These programs provide an understanding of alcohol addiction and resources and support to help cope. Please contact a local Alcoholics Anonymous program in your area. You can find local AA chapters by visiting *www.aa.org*. There are also others programs in addition to the AA chapters in your area you can look into as well. Please search the internet and find a program that suits you and your family's needs. Don't suffer with this addiction alone, get help and get help soon.

Embarrassment and shame may not seem like they come with an effect but they do; especially with children and young adults. This can lead to being bullied, which can lead to feelings of suicide. This can be the same affect with adults and can also lead to addictions in addition to alcohol, including drug use or other. The following is a link to the National Center for Victims of Crime and this website www.victimsofcrime.org has links to websites of various other support organizations, including some of those noted below:

1. The National Suicide Prevention Lifeline *http://www.suicidepreventionlifeline.org/* or call 1–800–273-TALK (8255). This is a 24/7 hotline.

2. Mothers Against Drunk Driving at *http://www. madd.org/* or call 1–877–275–6233.

3. The National Child Abuse Hotline at *https://www. childhelp.org/* or call 1–800–422–4453.

4. The National Domestic Violence Hotline at *http:// www.thehotline.org/* or call 1–800–799–7233 or 1–800–787–3224 (TTY).

5. National Indigenous Women's Resource Center *http://www.niwrc.org/about-us or call 855–649–7299*.

6. The National Runaway Switch Board *http:// www.1800runaway.org/* or call 1–800–786–2929 or text 66008.

7. Parents of Murdered Children at *http://www. pomc.org/* or call 1–888–818–7662.

8. Women's Law at *http://www.womenslaw. org/ or 1-800-799-7233* **NOTE:** *This is the same number to the National Domestic Hotline or TTY at* 1-800-787-3224.

Don't let the fear of what others think, stop you from getting the help you need. You are stronger than you may believe, and it takes a person of strength to admit they need help. There is no weakness, embarrassment or shame in reaching out for help. If you're facing challenges with any form of addiction, or just need to speak to someone, getting help is by far the best thing you can do for yourself.

I was not aware of such programs during the challenging times in my life. I thought the issues I was experiencing were normal and therefore, I thought it was just my lot in life. I thought I had to suck it up and keep going. Thank God that was not the case, or the truth. There is help available. Get help! It could make all the difference between life and death!

Questions:

1. Have you or anyone you know been sexually assaulted?

2. Have you or the person sought help or support to cope with the trauma of such an assault?

3. Have you or someone you know suffered physically abuse as a child?

4. Can you look back in your childhood and see where the separation of a parent is affecting your life as an adult?

5. Can you see where that experience is affecting your own intimate relationship, or your relationship with others?

6. Did you know separation from a parent can possibly cause a child to experience symptoms of grief?

7. Are you suffering from some form of addiction, such as alcoholism or another form?

If you have answered yes to the questions above, I earnestly urge you to seek God, and review the resources found in this book to get the help and support you may need.

Prayer

Father, I come beseeching you on behalf of the issues I identify with in this book. I am asking you to first give me peace, Father. Being raped is a very painful experience and can be traumatizing. Help me to accept the truth so I can be made free from the bondage of this experience, for your word say's in John 8:32 *"And ye shall know the truth, and the truth shall make you free."* Help me to understand and accept it was not my fault. Surround me in your love, a love which is faithful, eternal and complete. Give me the strength, guidance and empower me to seek the help that I need. Take away the images and the reminders that would try and hold me hostage to the experience, but grant me shalom (peace) Father to move past the experience. Through the power of your Holy Spirit; lead, guide and direct me in the way that I should go, to receive the help and support I will need, to get through this experience, and to live a life full of happiness and one of purpose. I thank you in advance and I seal this prayer in Jesus' powerful name, Amen!

Father, I understand alcoholism is a spirit of bondage and that I must pray and fast to break this spirit in my love one and I. I also understand Lord, that my love one and I may be drinking due to issues and circumstances we don't know how to handle in our own strength. I pray for my love one and I today, Lord. I pray you would break the yolks of past hurts and demonic strongholds that may have gripped us and brought forth this spirit of bondage. I ask you to break the spirit of pride that keeps us in hiding and from facing the truth. Destroy its power in our lives Father God through the name that is above every name, Jesus Christ! Strip the desire to drink. Take the desire and numb the taste buds of alcohol. Remove the natural and chemical imbalances that causes the body to yearn for alcohol, Father God. Remove any and all relationships—friendships and acquaintances—that would cause stumbling during the process of deliverance. Place in our path those who can boldly and scripturally encourage and strengthen us. We ask this in Jesus name! Amen!

Chapter Four

You Can Run, but You Can't Hide from Your Past, Your Present, or Your Future

*"Surely the Lord G*OD *will do nothing, but he revealeth his secret unto his servants the prophets."*

Amos 3:7

The Day She Died

After having brain surgery and being in a coma for two months, my mother was transferred to hospice care where she passed away. I remember the day I learned she had passed away like it was yesterday. She had been in the hospital a while prior to her passing and I wanted to make her proud of me. I had convinced myself she would recover, so while she was "recovering," I made up my mind I was going to do my best in school. It wasn't that I was bad in school, but I was trying everything I knew to ensure God would allow my mother to live. Unfortunately for me and for my siblings my efforts could not, and did not change the inevitable outcome for my mother. At the time of my mother's death, I was living with my best friend and her family. This particular morning, we were getting ready to leave for school. Every detail of this day I can remember so clearly. I remember the layout of the house they lived in, where I slept and exactly what I was doing that morning. I can remember every single detail!

We were almost ready to leave for school when my grandfather's truck pulled up. When I went to the front door and saw my grandmother walking towards me, I could see the look on her face and I knew why she was there. I looked up to the sky—I remember it being so blue, so pretty—and I screamed as loud as I could, "NOOOOOOOO!" I sobbed, I sobbed, I sobbed. I had never felt such pain before. My Lord, I was hurting! As I write this section of the book, my heart is heavy and my eyes well with tears and I'm thinking, mama! To think that after all of these years; I am forty-nine years old and I still miss her, terribly! As an adult woman, I still grieve the loss of my mother. Over the years, I have learned grief can last for a very long period of time. I've learned you can function normally in life and grieve at the same time.

I am still saddened by her not being here. I am saddened by all of the things I never had the opportunity of experiencing with her. I am saddened she was not there for my first wedding; to share in that nineteen-year relationship, or help me transition through the difficulty and pain of the divorce. She was not there to encourage me as I took that leap of faith into my second marriage; to assure me I was making the right choice, and to promise me as she gently stroked my cheek with the back of her hand, that the second marriage was a sure thing. She was not there to share in my accomplishment of passing my GED test with flying colors after being out of school for fifteen years! She missed me walking across the stage to received my certification from graphic design school. She was not there when I received my certification in business management, business writing, or personal finances. She was not here when I got my first job or moved into my first apartment. She was not there to see all of my accomplishments in corporate America; to tell me how proud she was of me at the promotions I received. She was not there when I started my first business, was anointed as a Prophetess, received my license as a minister or to see me minister in the pulpit for the first time! Nor, was she there to hold my hand and dry my tears when due to an ectopic pregnancy I lost my first child and the second time, when I miscarried alone in my bed. Why was I not allowed to experience all of these things with my mother lovingly by my side? The answers to these questions, like the zillions of others I've had rolling around in my head, I may never know. I have come to a beautiful resolve and peaceful acceptance that God knows what's best for me, and in him I have confidently put all of my trust. I will always love my mother and I still miss her with all of my heart!

SIDE BAR: *To all of the mothers and daughters, please don't take for granted, the blessings you are to each other. I personally find it difficult to understand how a mother can have her daughter or daughter's and don't spend time with them. Man, what I would give to have my mother. Or for that matter, daughters, who don't see their mothers for years. I would be on the phone with my mother all the time. Of course, this is being said after experiencing not having my mother. Perhaps, this gives me a little insight, since I know the void of not having my mother. Please take note. It leaves you with a huge void and it's never really filled again! Be mindful and ever so grateful and appreciative if you still have your mother.*

SIDE BAR: *The National Alliance for Grieving Children "promotes awareness of the needs of children and teens grieving a death and provides education and resources for anyone who wants to support them." You can learn more* *or find grief support in your area by visiting their website at https://childrengrieve.org/.*

And So They Begin Again

A short while before my mother's passing, I dreamt of her funeral. I saw her casket and what she was wearing; I saw everything and her actual service was just as I saw it in the dream. Imagine being a sixteen-year-old girl having dreamt of your mother's funeral. Imagine, if you will, having had dreams since a young child and by now at the age of sixteen, you know what you've seen in a night vision (a dream) was going to happen. I knew in the inner most parts of me this was going to happen and I was horrified at losing my mother, but what could I do. Scared none of my friends would believe me if I shared it, or worse, the possibility they would think I was crazy; I kept this information to myself.

While this fear was hidden deep within me, I went on hanging out with friends trying to ignore as best I could what I knew was the inevitable. I functioned in fear and anticipation of my mother's passing and I could not share what I saw, or what I knew with anyone. Imagine that, a teenager suffering alone. Sadly, while each occurrence is different, the tragedy is that the scenario of teenagers suffering alone, is an all too common one. How many are doing that today and turning to drugs, alcohol and other things to cope with what they don't understand?

Because of this dream about my mother's death, my dreams scared me until the mid-90s. They scared me because what I dreamt was no longer a dream, it was me seeing what was going to happen. Prior to the dream of my mother's funeral, I had awakened to what surely sounded like my mother's voice telling me to close the patio door and to lock it. Now this is significant because at the time I dreamt this, my mother lied in a coma in the hospital. The next morning upon waking, I learned from local news reports there had been a serial rapist in our area who was breaking into homes through unlocked patio doors and sexually assaulting the women residents.

This was not the first dream or vision I've had of things that would later reveal themselves in reality; this would actually be the beginning of many more dreams, visions, seeing writings on the walls, and more. I can remember the very details of most of my dreams/visions or spiritual insights, if you will. There is one I will never forget and it happened when I was about eight years old. I dreamt or had a vision of Jesus appearing in my mother's living room and he was positioned in the corner of the ceiling and he beckoned me with his index finger to come (he was calling me) and without saying a word he told me to not be afraid.

The dream, or vision shifted and now we are in the front of my elementary school and my classmates are all yelling "the sky is falling, the sky is falling" and I look up and there's this hand descending from the clouds. Another shift in the dream happens and now the hand is ascending back into heaven and I am now centered in the palm of the hand, along with many of my classmates. I never saw their faces, but somehow I knew they were my classmates.

Having had dreams and visions since I was about six or seven years old, they were not unfamiliar to me.

However, at that time and age, I thought the dreams and visions were nightmares. I imagine most children at this age would do the same. I believed they were nightmares because of this one particular dream I had repeatedly. It was of some men who were always trying to kill me. The shocking thing about this dream, or vision was the men carried machetes and they were lashing out at me with them, but they could never get passed the foot of my bed; regardless of their many attempts. I could remember screaming for my grandmother as loud as I could, but she would never come to my aide.

Looking back, what would I as a child know about dreams and visions, and their relevancy to my life and the to the lives of others. As time went on and I continued to dream more, I started to recognize the patterns of my dreams. Meaning those that required prayer to avert danger, those that required prayer to cope with the outcome, and those that required prayer to seek further understanding. I did not understand all of them, but over the years I have learned to recognize what approach to take regarding each dream. Much later, I would learn they would be key to me discovering who I was and what my purpose in life was. They would be key to me learning and accepting the call on my life. We'll pick my dreaming up again in a few chapters. Hold on to what you have read so far. I know, that was a hard dip. I promise, we'll pick them up again and right where I left off here. Keep reading.

Finally, I Felt Like I Belonged

A short time after my mother was laid to rest, I caught a bus to the Central Valley, where for the first time I met my father, his wife, my two sisters, and two brothers. During this visit I was also able to meet my two uncles, my aunt, my great aunt, my grandmother, and great-grandmother. I also met some of my cousins on my father's side. They were all so loving and accepting of me and I felt right at home, amongst family. I never once felt like a stepsister or my father's other child and I attribute that to my father, but mostly to his wife, my stepmom.

I will never forget stepping off that bus knowing exactly who he was; it was the greatest feeling ever.

Finally, I felt like I belonged, like I knew who I was. The missing piece to the puzzle was now in place. I was no longer missing a significant part of my life. All of the stories I had heard of him were now a reality for me. I was never told anything negative about my father as a child. Even when I was told he denied me, it was not with a negative connotation. I had always heard how I looked just like him, was gifted and talented just like him, and had the gift of singing like him (that part is not altogether true). I can sing a lil bit, but he could *sang*, seriously! Big difference! Even though I had just lost my mother, looking up at this six foot tall man I felt safe, secure, and complete! I felt loved. He was my new hero!

SIDE BAR: *Fathers, your daughters need you. You are relevant to their development, to their identity, to their self-esteem and self-worth. You are relevant to the woman they become! You have* an impact on the legacy they establish and leave to their children. *Be more than* *present, be involved, be committed, and be the example of the man worthy of your princess! Sister's the same goes for us as daughters of God. God desires us to have the man/the mate, he created us to be the "helpmeet" to. We must stop settling for less than God desires for us!*

The visit to my father's house forever changed my life. Now that I look back upon the timing I realized it was perfect. That sounds odd I know. The loss of my mother could have been much more devastating than it was had I not been given the opportunity to meet my father. Now don't get me wrong, the loss of my mother was very painful and no sixteen-year-old child should have to experience that level of pain. However, the love and perfect timing of God is so awesome that he saved me from what could have been a hell of a time for me. That level of pain could have launched me into rebellion, drugs, numerous unhealthy relationships and so much more. Instead, the love and acceptance I felt from my father, stepmother, siblings and other relatives were a life saver for me. God always has a RAM in the bush so to speak, and it is never what we could have imagined.

The Impressions We Leave

This time in my life also brought some fun and memorable times for me; they brought some much needed smiles and laughter to my damaged spirit and fragile soul. I can remember being in the kitchen with my stepmom and how loving she was and she still is to this day. I can still see her beautiful smile standing in that kitchen and I can still sense her calm and peaceful demeanor. It's funny, when thinking of her I still get that peaceful and calm feeling. Up until she reads this book, I don't believe she ever knew what I experienced prior to coming to her home. It was her I often looked back on when I found myself faced with a similar situation as a woman. It was how she showed nothing but acceptance and love and how she never treated me any different than the other kids. Even as a young adult, the impact of this experience had a lifelong effect on me. She showed nothing short of grace and pure love and for that I will be forever grateful.

Each time I stayed with them she taught me how to love by example. It was not in what she said, but in what she did without ever saying a word. She taught me how a real woman carries herself. She showed me the power of inner strength and beauty. Ladies, do you see the power we as women have if used correctly? Do you see the impact we can have on the lives and purposes of children, and their destiny?

My stepmom did not know what I would do or what I would become. She did not know I would be writing this book; neither did I for that matter. She did not and until the reading of this book, probably never imagined I felt this way or viewed her the way I have all of these years. Imagine if she had treated me differently than she did and had done so not knowing what I had gone through. How would or could my experience with her and my father have changed the course and direction of my life? I earnestly pray that we as women pay careful attention to the influence and power we have. Not only with our children and spouses, but in the world as a whole. Dare I remind us of all the women in the bible who had significant impacts on the history and some of the effects of their actions? Just to mention a few: Ruth, Naomi, Queen Esther and Mary, the mother of Jesus.

What had been a nice welcome and short visit with my father and family had left an impact on me that was life-changing. The visit was over and now I had to return to living with my grandmother and my family in Los Angeles. I was now back to the reality of what happened and the questions are starting to flood my mind once again. The truth that I was not the child that left my grandmother's house some three years earlier was resurfacing. I was now seventeen and had witnessed more in the last three years than most children my age witness all their teen years combined.

The Jolt of Reality

I had just loss my mother after fighting for three years to try and save her life; me a sixteen-year-old girl. In addition to everything else, and during the last year and a half prior to my mother's death, I myself was involved in a relationship with a young man who was as wholesome as they come and as sweet as pie. He was brought up in a very nice home, his family was nice and me, as messed up as I was, I was able to catch his attention and capture his heart. He was what every young girl dreamed of and every mother dreamed of for her child. My mother and grandmother knew him and they both approved of him and loved him.

To this day, I am not sure he knew everything going on in my twisted life, but what he did know, he was patient, kind, tolerant and understanding. His family was so family oriented, something I didn't have and I loved spending time with them. Sometime shortly before or after my mother's death, I can't recall exactly when, our relationship ended. I learned during this time in my life that people who are hurt, usually end up hurting others.

With all that I had gone through, I learned the all too common practice of keeping secrets. I was really fearful of what people would think of me if they knew all I was experiencing. I felt somehow guilty that what my mom and I were experiencing was somehow my fault. Maybe if she didn't have me, she would not have gone through all she went through. Maybe I was causing too much pressure for her? The shame of it all caused me to now start keeping secrets and for a while, I thought I was doing darn good at it. I was functioning with a big smile on my face, laughing with friends, socializing, hanging out and appearing to enjoy myself, all while I was dealing with everything I was dealing with on the inside.

SIDE BAR: *Children really do mimic what they see. They really do learn by example. Regardless if those examples are positive or negative, they do learn. We must be very careful of the life lessons we are teaching our children by our actions.*

I am sure there were a few people who knew what was really going on with me and my mother. Unfortunately, those who did know could not offer any assistance to us. Including the alcoholic friends of my mother's, who were most likely too drunk to even process anything, let alone offer assistance. There were also the so-called boyfriends of my mothers, the very men who were taking advantage of me, who knew what was going on, since they were doing what they were doing. Sometimes my mother's drinking would cause her to have a skewed understanding and she would get angry. I would have to hold my mother down to prevent her from trying to fight me while she was drunk. It hurt me to have to do this, but after being beat by her with the heels of her shoes in my eyes while drunk, I had to. I would be asking her to "just stop. Please, just stop and sit down!"

There would be times when I would see men trying to take advantage of her. The entire experience was sad. It's really unfortunate that I was taught through these experiences how to bear pain, shame, guilt, and keep going. You didn't say anything; that was life as I knew it. But even though this is what I was exposed to, I knew something was not right, because at my grandmother's house, this was not the experience I was having. I wonder how many more women learned this lesson as a child and carried it into their adulthood?

SIDE BAR: *It's easy for us to look at a woman, a woman who may be on the streets, a woman who is a heavy drinker, someone who abuses drugs, or who is promiscuous and judge her, but as I have noted throughout this book, have we stopped to consider the "Why Factor?" There is always a cause and an effect to everything. Let's not be so quick to judge, but let's try and be more understanding and do so in wisdom and with compassion.*

It may not mean to take a drug addict into your home and risk losing all of your possessions. Be prayerful and wise about the course of action you take. Be led of the Spirit of God before you move out in action. Offering assistance, or support may not mean take a woman into your home who will in no doubt seduce your spouse; again, use Godly wisdom. Using wisdom does not mean we don't offer help, or support. Any type of help, or support should begin with consideration of what the situation calls for and as noted above, we should always inquire in prayer before proceeding.

Now, back at my grandmother's house I did not dare tell her any of what I had experienced, including that I had been raped and molested. In fact, as noted earlier, I just told her I had experienced sexual abuse prior to the release of this book and I'm forty-nine years old and she's eighty-five years old. Talk about keeping secrets.

When I returned to my grandmother's house would she be expecting that thirteen-year-old granddaughter of hers to return? The one who cried out to her to come and get me one cold night, the night we left my mother passed out on the floor. If so, I am sorry; that child cannot return to her. She doesn't exist anymore. I am now a sexually violated young girl. One who had been sexually assaulted by my mother's boyfriends, a family member and a so-called family friend. Not only am I scarred by these experiences, I am held captive by the fear; a fear that has restricted me from telling my grandmother all I had experienced while I was away from her.

I am now a teenager, dealing with my own "teenage issues" and tormented by horrific experiences and painful memories my young and confused mind can't even begin to comprehend. That girl who left my grandmother's home three years earlier, really doesn't' exist anymore. Her childhood was damaged long before she left the first time, and her innocence was robbed from her during this three-year period and can never be returned to her. And now, returning and having to try and adjust . . . this was an impossible task, and one my grandmother would never understand because she would never know what happened to me to be able to properly help me.

Adjusting Is Never Easy

Well, I tried to adjust to my new life as best I could. I got into school immediately and tried to resume with some sense of normalcy. I wanted to finish school and still make my mother proud of me, even though she had passed on. I was always a determined child and I had learned from living with my mother how to make the best out of many bad situations. With the experiences of living with other people, I tried to decorate their houses and make them nice, even though they were shacks because most of the people where alcoholics. Even in the motels, I tried to make them nice by keeping them clean. So I took that same attitude and approach to try and make the best out of where I currently found myself. Not that my grandmother's house was a shack. I meant learning how to adjust to change.

How do I deal with all that has just happened in my life? I mean from losing my mother and everything during the last three years of her life, to meeting my father and his side of the family for the first time. To learning how to adjust to living with my grandmother again and trying to act like a normal seventeen-year-old girl. How do I do all of this? I've never known what being a normal child, or teenager was like from the beginning? How do I go from being forced to be an adult with adult responsibilities, to being the protector of my siblings, to trying to handle and understand my mother's death and the effect it would have on my sister and my brothers, to trying to adjust to life without her? What will her death mean to and for us, the children left behind? I had more questions than I had answers, all while my life was taking yet another dramatic turn.

What about my baby brother, my mother's last child? When we last saw him, he was one-years old. We did not see him again for 5-years. That was when his dad brought him to see my mother and us. This was a short time before my mother's passing, talk about timing. I often thought about what, if anything, would he remember about his mother and of us, his siblings? What would my other brother, my mother's first born son and my little sister remember of her? If they did remember, what would their memories of her be?

I often thought about these things, and in all honesty, no seventeen-year-old girl should've had to carry such a burden, but I did. I am now considering all of this while trying to adapt to a life I will now have to live without my mother. In my mind I am trying to make sense of everything that has taken place, but how can I? Why did I have to suffer with her the last three years of her life? How cruel is that for a child to endure? Why did I have to see and experience everything I had seen and experienced? What was the purpose of it all? Was there a purpose for it all?

SIDE BAR: *I imagined Joseph in the bible had some of the same questions. Questions like, why did I have to grow up with such hatred and jealousy among my own brothers? Why did I have to be singled out by my Father and notably so as his favorite, the one chosen to be the next heir? Why did God allow my brothers to throw me in a ditch and sell me into slavery? Why did I have to be falsely accused of sexual assault and thrown into a prison dungeon?*

Why, Lord? What do you think his thoughts were after being placed second in charge in Egypt during the time of the famine and when his family would need him most? The word of God tells us in Romans 8:28 "And we know that all things work together for good to them that love God, to them who are the called according to his purpose."

God's word also reminds us in 1 Peter 4:12 of this fact "Beloved, think it not strange concerning the fiery trial which is to try you, as though some strange thing happened unto you." I am sure most of you reading this book questioned some of the things you experienced, as I have. I sum it all up by agreeing with the Word. Think it not strange, as all things are working together...

Back to Trying to Adjust

In an effort to move on with my life the best way I knew, I buried everything deep in the depths of my mind. I locked it up and decided to never open it again. At the age of thirteen, I was learning the art to "grin and bear it." I mean there are literally things I cannot remember, including some people. I did not know that with such traumatic experiences, you could block certain memories. In doing a little research to try and understand why my sister, who is four years younger, could recall "specific details" that I simply could not remember. That is until she triggered my memory to the event.

My research revealed this is referred to as *"Suppressed Memory."* The below reference comes from an article written in the Stanford Report (Stanford University) *"The big news is that we've shown how the human brain blocks an unwanted memory, that there is such a mechanism and it has a biological basis," said Stanford psychology Professor John Gabrieli, a co-author of the paper titled "Neural Systems Underlying the Suppression of Unwanted Memories." "It gets you past the possibility that there's nothing in the brain that would suppress a memory—that it was all a misunderstood fiction."*

"The experiment showed that people are capable of repeatedly blocking thoughts of experiences they don't want to remember until they can no longer retrieve the memory, even if they want to," Gabrieli explained. The complete article can be found and viewed on their website via the below link

http://news.stanford.edu/news/2004/january14/memory-114.html

There is also an article I read on *"Adult Survivors of Childhood Traumas"* as over the years I have thought about my past experiences and how I have dealt with them in my adult years, such as my determination to avoid the areas where most of these experiences took place, including not visiting my mother's grave site. The fact that over the years I have never really discussed the specifics with anyone; not even family and friends during or even after I had the experiences. I also didn't want to remember any of the people from my past or some of the specific places we lived. It's really strange you know; while I can recall the events and I know certain things took place, I don't recall perhaps the color of the walls, or the clothes being worn, or address of specific places. The power of the brain is pretty amazing. Below is a little bit of the article.

"Is it Possible to Forget Childhood Trauma?" "People forget names, dates, faces and even entire events all the time. But is it possible to forget terrible experiences such as being raped? Or beaten? The answer is yes—under certain circumstances. For more than a hundred years, doctors, scientists and other observers have reported the connection between trauma and forgetting. But only in

the past 10 years have scientific studies demonstrated a connection between childhood trauma and amnesia."

Most scientists agree that memories from infancy and early childhood—under the age of two or three—are unlikely to be remembered. Research shows that many adults who remember being sexually abused as children experienced a period when they did not remember the abuse. Scientists also have studied child victims at the time of a documented traumatic event, such as sexual abuse, and then measured how often the victims forget these events as they become adults. They discovered that some people do forget the traumatic experiences they had in childhood, even though it was established fact that the traumatic events occurred." This study/ article can be found on the "International Survivors of Childhood Trauma' s website via the following link *http://www.istss.org/public-resources/remembering-childhood-trauma.aspx.*

SIDE BAR: *Childhood trauma is real and affects us not only as children, but as adults!*

Now with the past and all of the pain securely locked away, I now have a redefined goal of making something of my life. I made a determination that all that I saw would not become my reality, my life, nor my legacy. Besides, growing up as the oldest grandchild on my mother's side, my grandmother drilled it in me, that as the oldest grandchild, I needed to set the example for the other kids to follow. She started telling me this during one of the times I lived at her house. I was probably about eight, or nine years old. So armed with these words and my past experiences, I set out to be something and to accomplish something in my life. I was determined not to be a product of my environment.

Now, back in school and trying to keep my recent past buried, I thrust myself into many different things. I started thinking of what I wanted to be and do. I decided I wanted to become a nurse because I did not like the care my mother was receiving when hospitalize. I recall some of the times, not all of them, when I would go to visit her and the condition I would sometimes find her in was not satisfactory to me. I wanted her skin to be moist and well-conditioned. I wanted those providing care to massage her hands that were crooked, as a result of the emergency brain surgery the doctors said she needed.

I wanted them to brush her hair as it grew back from them having to shave her head to conduct the brain surgery. I wanted them to keep her lips moist with vaseline, or chap stick. I could not stand to visit and find her the way I sometimes did. It's not that they weren't providing the best care, perhaps it was the fact that I was her daughter, her sixteen-year-old daughter who did not understand adult situations, or medical practices. Perhaps I did not understand medically what could be done and what could not be done. Perhaps I was just going through so much emotionally that I could not comprehend anything. Going to see her was bad enough, but watching her lay there, hands bent, head bald and teeth separated from the brain surgery and unaware anyone was even there. My God . . . no child should have to experience anything like this, ever!

Trauma Can Lead to Tragedy

Do you see what some children go through? Can you imagine the impact childhood experiences are having on adults? How, if not understood they can and will mold your life; affecting the decisions you make, including having an impact on any, and all future relationships? This information alone should help us take into consideration why some adults are the way they are. Since this is my life, let's continue to look at how all of this affected me as an adult? Well, in my young mind the care or lack of care my mother was receiving caused me to want to be a nurse. Maybe this was a way I could deal with the guilt of feeling like I let my mother down. Like I did not do enough to protect her, or she would not have died. Not having my father in my life during my childhood years and hearing stories growing up about his gift of singing among other gifts and talents he possessed, made me want to pursue a music career (go figure).

It was a way, my way to be connected to him. In my mind, having something he possessed, made me feel not only like I belonged somewhere in this world, but that I belonged to him, a real person! Something as simple as young adults not knowing what they want to do in life, appearing to be fickle or confused, can be a result of things they're experiencing. We must look deeper at what is happening in the lives of our children and be a little more patient and understanding. We must also be attentive, where possible in the lives of our adult loved ones. Emotionally, I was a seventeen-year-old confused child, who was all over the place as a result of the experiences I had. But God!

After going through all of the craziness during my last year in school, the desire I had to be a nurse was short lived. It was too soon after my mother's passing and too painful to pursue. I then turned to trying to pursue a singing career. I have always loved to sing and I absolutely loved music! I loved all types of music. I loved the different instruments and in particular, I loved the piano the most. Through my little sister I learned of this music group in Los Angeles that was scheduled to perform at her school and she needed a chaperone for the event.

She had established a crush on one of the lead singers. I escorted her to this event and we were able to get close enough to the groups limo where I was able to meet and share my telephone number with the member she had the crush on. Long story short, we met each other and eventually became friends. The end result would be me meeting his family and him meeting mine. Our families ended up having a deeper connection that we would later discover.

Sometime later the group disbanded and the two of us decided to create a male and female group that would be the "first" male and female group where both members sung and also rapped. We actually had studio recording sessions, performed at a venue or two in the greater Los Angeles area and we worked with a well-known radio station in Los Angeles who was helping to promote and market us. We had a good thing and it really could have worked, but I was just too messed up. Eventually, due to my past that he knew very little, if anything about, our efforts did not last long and while our friendship did not end the group did when I informed him of my decision to relocate. Unfortunately, this was a very confusing time for me. I did not know what I wanted, who I was and what my life meant anymore. At times I felt like I was in outer space somewhere trying to grasp a hold to anything that made sense, to anything that seemed normal.

After a year of living with my grandmother, having enrolled in school trying to be a normal seventeen-year-old child and being on the LA scene trying to get into the music industry, I could not take it anymore. It all became too much and I felt like I needed to get away. I was having a hard time adjusting to living with my grandmother and my family. There was nothing wrong with my family, it was everything that was wrong with me. It seemed my family had changed, just as dramatic as my life with my mother had changed.

Nothing was the same any more. As a child, I recalled living in specific areas in Los Angeles and during those times having a normal childhood where things were great and where my grandmother and aunts were great role models. Now for the second time, we are living in one of the worst projects in Los Angeles. Coming home from school and walking through the projects, I had grown men whistling at me when I got off the bus (A painful reminder), boys trying to flirt with me and calling me out of my name if I did not respond. Girls being jealous of me and wanting to fight me just because of how I looked, the color of my skin and the texture of my hair. At seventeen, I had had enough of it all; the fighting, the violence, having a gun pulled on me in the projects, the rape and molestations, the alcohol drinking, the teasing and being made fun of, the broken heart, the loss of my mother, the inability to finish school; all of it. It was simply too much drama . . . enough was enough. After all of that, I was looking for and wanting a way out. I needed a way of escape. All of the trauma in my life was now becoming tragic!

With many questions floating around in my head, I could not help but think how many girls get caught up in sex trafficking, prostitution, unhealthy relationships, drug addictions, physically abusive relationships, and more—all because they're trying to find a way out! They are wooed by false promises of freedom, hope, and a better life. And to think, all they want is to simply get out. Me, I wanted to go to college out of State. I wanted to graduate and be a lawyer. I wanted to help the under-privileged, the underdog, so to speak. Why me? Why my life? It's interesting what happens to you when enough is enough? When you can't take it anymore? What happens to you when all you want to do is escape, to get out and get away? What happens is the opportunity presents itself, the question is, do you take it? I received a phone call that forever shifted my life and placed me on a course for God's will to be done in my life. You can run, but you can't hide from your past, your present, or your future.

Key Points:

- Where does the child who may have a special spiritual gift from God go for support and understanding? Those who see dreams, visions and other spiritual signs. Those who try and tell their parents what's going on with them and the parent cast if off as insignificant? What are we doing to them? Where are we forcing them to go and seek help and understanding? Are we sending them to the sorcerers, tara card readers and/or the psychic hotline for answers?

- Let me assure you, the spirit realm is real and our children are tapping into this realm and bad things are happening as a result. We must pay attention to the early signs before they drift into a darkness they may not so easily recover from, if at all.

- Many children today are walking around in fear of the things currently occurring in their homes and with peer pressure they hold it in. Could this be why our children are turning to dark music and violent games to vent and relieve their frustrations?

- What happens to the child who doesn't want to go home to avoid experiencing the violence of an intoxicated parent from alcohol or a strung out parent on drugs, or to see their parents fighting? Could this be a reason kids begin doing drugs so early in their lives? Could these be some of the reasons our children are incapable of handling the plethora of emotions going on inside of them?

• Women, please consider the facts, whether or not we set out to be role models, or not, we are role models to those who are around us. To those who watch us on T.V. To those who listen to our music. To those who read our books. To those who watch our performances. To those who watch us period! We must be mindful!

• We all know the old saying "kids imitate what they see," need I say more? How we speak. How we dress. How we display confidence, or the lack there of. How we demonstrate self-respect, or the lack there of. We are being watched and mimicked, rather we choose to be or not.

• The daughter, young girl or young woman you see, is the result of the mother, mentor or unknown, unaware mentor/woman you portrayed before them. We must consider what level of influence we are having regardless if it is intended or not. We have responsibility.

- A lot of times we look at the young girls, teenagers and young women and we judge them without ever giving thought to what may have thrusted them into where they are. What caused them to seek out an unhealthy relationship? What provoked them to want the pure and undefiled love of a baby, therefore finding themselves pregnant with no father and no way to sustain themselves, or their unborn child? These actions and more are not without cause. We must consider the why factor instead of judgement.

Resources:

1. Here is a link with data "Child Trends," this data shares information about the family structure *http://www.childtrends.org/?indicators=family-structure*

2. National Alliance for Grieving Children—The National Alliance for Grieving Children promotes

awareness of the needs of children and teens grieving a death and provides education and resources for anyone who wants to support them. Find out more about the NAGC by vising their website at https://childrengrieve.org/about-us

3. Stanford University (The Stanford Report on Suppressed Memory). Read the full article by visiting their website at *http://news.stanford.edu/ news/2004/january14/memory-114.html.*

4. International Society for Traumatic Stress Studies provided and article on Adult Survivors of Childhood Trauma and you can read the full article by visiting their website at *http://www. istss.org/public-resources/remembering-child-hood-trauma.aspx*

Questions:

1. Have you experienced dreams in your life that seemed like they had significance? If so, have you sought God about this experience? Journal all of

your dreams and certainly pray about them and ask God for clarity and understanding. If God is giving them, there is certainly a reason and a purpose. NOTE: Before I go to bed at night, I have learned to pray a specific prayer, asking God to take authority over every dream and vision, that none be given, unless given my him.

2. Have you thought about the impact you as a woman have had on a young girl in your sphere of influence? If not, pay attention to how those around you are mimicking you and consider how you feel about what they are not only seeing in you, but doing because of you.

3. Is your daughter, or son finding it difficult to adapt? Are you seeing signs They are changing; eating habits, new or changed group of friends, or lack of friends, new habits being formed? Pay attention to changes and seek the necessary help if needed. Don't ignore the warning signs?

4. Is your daughter trying to escape pain or depressing thoughts? Escaping does not have to

be literal. It can be escaping through drinking, using drugs, getting involved in an unhealthy relationship, joining a gang, cutting herself, establishing uncommon or new friendships, suffering from eating disorders such as bulimia, anorexia and more? If you notice any of the signs noted, please reach out for help.

Prayer:

Father, as I am reading this book, I or my loved one is experiencing things that seem uncommon in the spiritual realm, such as dreams and visions of things to come. I pray that you would first remove any and all fear and confusion, Father God. Your word declares that you did not give us a spirit of fear, but of peace, love, and of a sound mind. I ask that my loved one or I would become more intimate with you so these things would no longer be uncommon. I pray you would reveal the origination, purpose and revelatory knowledge of each experience, just as you gave Daniel and the four

Hebrew boys in Daniel 1:17, *"As for these four children, God gave them knowledge and skill in all learning and wisdom: and Daniel had understanding in all visions and dreams."* Confirm every dream or vision Father, through your word. There are many who speak falsely according to your word in 1 John 4:1, *"Beloved, believe not every spirit, but try the spirits whether they are of God: because many false prophets are gone out into the world."* Grant peace and comfort to know you are in control of what is revealed. Remove the "spooky" connotation and allow my loved one or me to see just how honorable the gift of prophecy is. For your word says in Amos 3:7, *"Surely the Lord God will do nothing, but he reveaLETh his secret unto his servants the prophets."* I pray you would keep me or my loved one humble before you. I pray against the spirit of pride and arrogance that may attempt to rise up in me or my loved one. I ask this all in Jesus Holy Name, Amen!

Father, I pray for the fathers to be present in the homes and in the lives of their children. I pray for the structure of the home to be as you designed it to be from the beginning. Your word says in Proverbs 22: 6, *"Train* up a child in the way he should go: and when he is old, he *will not depart from it.*" Let us conduct our families as you have ordained as noted in Ephesians 6:1–4, "*Children, obey your parents in the Lord: for this is right. Honour thy father and mother; which is the first commandment with promise; That it may be well with thee, and thou mayest live long on the earth. And, ye fathers, provoke not your children to wrath: but bring them up in the nurture and admonition of the Lord.*" I desire your word be honored in our home, Father. I pray that as a people we would come to repentance. Our world, country, state, cities, communities, and families are out of order, because we are out of Godly order. Help us to return to you with a repentant spirit, Father. You promised us in 2 Chronicles 7:14 "*If my people, which are called by my name, shall humble themselves, and pray, and seek my face, and turn from their wicked ways; then will I hear from heaven, and will forgive their sin, and will heal their land.*" Our land needs healing Lord, but we must first turn our face back to you. Create in us a clean heart and renew a right spirit within us. I ask this in Jesus' Precious Name, Amen!

Father, I am your daughter, created as a woman, and we have such powerful and significant influences in the lives of our children, our families, and our acquaintances; help me to use Godly wisdom in all of my affairs. Keep me mindful that I can sway our young women and others with how I conduct myself, as it is said in 2 Timothy 1:5, "*When I call to remembrance the unfeigned faith that is in thee, which dwelt first in thy grandmother Lois, and thy mother Eunice; and I am persuaded that in thee also.*" Help me to stay clear of ungodly behaviors that will cause me—and others—to stumble. Empower me to stand firmly on your word in James 4:7, which states "*Submit yourselves therefore to God. Resist the devil, and he will flee from you.*" Help me to see myself as the virtuous woman from Proverb 31; as Queen Esther, empowered to save her people; as Naomi, governing a young Ruth into her destiny; as Hannah, bringing forth the Prophet Samuel, who would anoint the 1st and 2nd Kings of Israel; and as Elizabeth, birthing a trailblazer who would set the pathway to our Lord and Savior Jesus Christ. Help me to see my significance, to see how powerful and very influential I am as a daughter of the most-high God. I AM SIGNIFICANT, POWERFUL AND VERY INFLUENTIAL. Help me to never use the honor bestowed upon me as your daughter in the wrong ways. Help me Lord, to honor you with what you have gifted me with, that in my journey of life, I will always live a life worthy of bringing glory and honor to your name. In Jesus' Sweet Name I pray, Amen!

Chapter 5

The Move, Not Quite What I Expected; the Wilderness Again

"Remember ye not the former things, neither consider the things of old. Behold, I will do a new thing; now it shall spring forth; shall ye not know it? I will even make a way in the wilderness, and rivers in the desert."

Isaiah 43:18–19

The Opportunity of a Life Time

A year had gone by since my mom's passing and I was living with my grandmother when I was offered an opportunity to move to Oakland, California. The offer came from someone I had a crush on from a very young age. The person was a member of the family I was living with at the time of my mom's passing. Our mothers were acquainted when my mother and I lived at another friend's house and they lived in the apartment across from us. It was during this time when our families became closely acquainted and when I first caught a glimpse of him.

When the offer came to relocate to Oakland, needless to say, I jumped at the opportunity to leave. I needed a break. I needed a change. I desperately needed to get away from everything that reminded me of the last three years of my life. I wanted to get away from everything that caused me pain; to get away from all of the nightmares that were associated with the events of the last three years. I saw an opportunity to flee and I took it! Is there anyone looking to flee in your circle? Pay attention, there could be warning signs!

At the time I was presented with this opportunity, I was only seventeen-years-old and just one month from my eighteenth birthday. After much pondering, I finally got up enough courage to ask my grandmother if I could move to Oakland. Surprisingly, she said yes. Perhaps she thought if she had said no, I would have left anyway. Well, that would not have happened. I respected my grandmother far too much and would never have left without her approval. To this day, I am not sure what or how she felt about all of this, or why she even said yes. But I suspect that after a year of watching me struggle first-hand, for whatever reason, she figured saying yes was the thing to do. I have never asked her why she said yes and I accept I will probably never know the answer.

I've often thought if I asked her, it would bring back a painful time in her life and I did not want to do that. This was a time where I had not only lost my mother, but a time where she had just lost her oldest daughter. A time where I, her first grandchild was preparing to move away. Imagine if you will, being her; being plagued with thoughts from the past, thoughts of this being an all too familiar scenario and the fear associated with it. I imagined she wondered if this could be history repeating itself. Was she thinking that like my mother who left home, that my life could end up like hers if I left too? Now, I can only imagine ohc would not want to see this, or ever want to go through such an experience again. Being a seventeen-year-old young girl, with issues and a desire to flee, I was not thinking responsibly.

In my so-called preparation to relocate, I don't recall many conversations about the move taking place between my boy-friend and I. Questions that mature adults would ask; questions about our plans for the future, our careers, and furthering our education were not discussed. There was only wooing. So it took very little effort for me to move to Oakland.

SIDE BAR: Can you see from my experience that when a young girl is in "flee mode" we ignore signs of caution, we don't consider our options, the consequences, or the results of our choices. We are operating on a one-track mind, one that says get me out of here and get me out of here fast! That's all we're thinking about and the decisions we make in those moments can be life altering and perhaps not in the ways we may have imagined.

Oakland, Here I Come

Once in Oakland, my life would never be the same. On the night of September 6, 1984, I waited patiently for my grandmother, who was in the bathroom to come out so I could say good-bye, but she never did. She kissed me before she went in and maybe that was her plan all along so she would not have to see me walk out the door. After waiting a while, my grandfather gathered all of my belongings and loaded them into his pick-up truck and we left for downtown Los Angeles, headed to the Greyhound bus station.

As I write this passage, I am recalling a conversation I recently had with my grandmother about the night I left. She told me that seeing me leave was too painful for her. I looked at her face, some thirty years later, I could see the pain as she reflected on that night. What is so incredibly amazing is that she is suffering from the onset of Dementia and still, she was able to go back to that specific night and recall what she felt. As she reflected on that night and the pain she felt, it made me sad for

179

a moment. Now I knew, that my suspicions were correct. To ask her why she said yes would only bring her more pain.

SIDE BAR: *Children, you don't know the pain you cause your parents about decisions you make. Parents are not impenetrable. Their hearts hurt for you in ways you will never understand until perhaps you yourself become a parent. For my grandmother, I now know that it was painful for her to see me leave and that night, my grandfather suggesting we leave so I would not miss my bus was, I'm sure for her benefit as well as mine. He orchestrated the night's events perfectly. I can only imagine the pain in his heart as he anticipated leaving my grandmother in the emotional state she was in, while considering how to console her when he returned home. I never once thought about how my grandmother felt with my leaving. As I write this, it makes my heart heavy, because I love her so much and I would never want to cause her any sort of pain. Children, you really don't know the pain you cause your parents in the decisions you make. Please, be mindful!*

Off we went. We made it to the bus station on time and my grandfather saw to it that I made it on the bus safely and provided me with some much-needed advice before he left me to board my bus. I can still see his face and how he looked at me as he got off the bus. I can still remember his walk and how he spoke. He was not my grandfather by blood, but he was my grandfather. He believed in me. He never said it, but it was what he did that showed me he believed in me. It was in his own way that he encouraged me. I miss him so much!

Well, I am now on the bus and lo and behold, I was on my way to Oakland, California. After a long eleven-and-a-half-hour bus ride, I had arrived in downtown Oakland. I was so excited to be starting my new life. On the long bus ride I thought about all the years I had carried this crush; since I was a little girl. My mind was racing and I thought for sure in order for someone to ask you to relocate and move where they are, surely they must have had feelings for you, right?

All night long I thought about what life was going to be like for us. Would we have kids? Would we get married?

Would we get a house together? There were so many thoughts this eleven-and-a-half hour bus ride yielded. With so many thoughts, hopes and dreams filling my mind for a better life and the anticipation and the excitement of seeing him, I was exhausted from the long ride. Ready or not, at 6:30 a.m. on Friday, September 7, 1984 my bus pulls into a gloomy and overcast Oakland. It was time for my new life! We greet each other, loaded the car with my life in a few suitcases, and we head towards the 580 freeway on our way to what would be my new home and my new life.

Prior to my arriving, he lined up a job for me working at his grandmother's board and care home. I'm not sure what he told her to 1) get her to agree to my moving to Oakland and 2) to my working at her board and care home. Whatever he told her, she agreed to both. His grandmother was mean and she scared the living daylights out of me. But underneath all that meanness was the most caring person you would ever meet. She was the one who helped me establish my first bank account. She was the one who took me to get my driver's license. It was she who helped me to get certified as a Home Health Aide and it was she who helped me get my first retail job. Things were looking up for me. I did it! I was starting to make a path for me that was the total opposite of what I had recently left behind. At least, so it seemed.

The beginning of my new transition was beautiful. We were having so much fun together. We both were huge baseball fans and we would attend lots of baseball games together and it was a lot of fun. I have always been a huge sports fan, so this was right up my alley. We were hanging out with his friends and I was meeting their wives and girlfriends and developing friendships with them. Of course, I was the youngest of them all. Thinking back now, I can't help but imagine what these women were thinking about me. Probably somewhere along the lines of "this poor baby." He showed me around, educating me on the do's and don'ts of Oakland. The places I could go and the places I should not go. He showed me how to catch the BART train and more; he was acclimating me to life in Oakland.

It was not long before I was introduced to his family and friends. They all welcomed me into the family and took me under their wing. The older ladies were instrumental in helping me to adjust to my new life. We would go to family gatherings for the holidays and it was great. I thought, surely, this was the life I had desired all along. I thought I had made it. I made it through the difficult times. I made it through all of the hell and my life was now on the right track. Ceola was on the road to making something of her life. How about that.

Life Teaches Us Lessons, Ready or Not

What I did not know was life was about to teach me some serious "life" lessons! I was about to learn that fun times only last so long. I was about to learn that life was real, not a fantasy full of fun and always happy times. I was about to learn that life had seasons. I was about to learn just how much I did not know about life. I was going to learn how to deal with living with a man and all that comes with that; the emotional trauma, how to balance my own life along with that of another person. There was so much I didn't know. I thought I was ready, but to tell you the truth, I was nowhere near ready for what I was about to experience.

Over the course of the next seven years "life school" was in and I am ever so grateful for his grandmother during this time. She would teach me a lot, until her death in the early 90's. I'm grateful for the things she took the time to teach me in her own unique way. For how tough she was on me and for how she challenged me. All of this was crucial in my adjustment and in my maturing. What a beautiful, tough, and I believe sometimes misunderstood woman, but truly loving in her own way. I will forever be grateful for her.

Now my grandmother taught me the basics; she taught me how to cook everything from scratch, how to clean and keep a home, how to keep myself as a woman, and how to grocery shop. She also taught me other life skills, including the importance of having good morals, values, and integrity. She was not able to teach me how to handle an intimate relationship and to live with a man, or how to handle my emotions. Nor was she able to teach me how to deal with the pain of a broken heart and how to bounce back from a broken spirit. Because of my childhood, she was not able to teach me or better yet, help me to understand how to survive a crushed soul. How could my grandmother teach me such things? These are all things only life could teach through living life and learning from each experience. Had I stayed at home with her longer, she could have better prepared me for what "real life" brings to the table.

SIDE BAR: *Young ladies, please don't be so quick to flee. You just might be running to a situation worse than the one you're trying so desperately to escape. There is something to the cliché we all know so well "the grass always appears greener on the other side." Consider all of your options before you leave and make sure your decision is made after seeking wise counsel and much prayer.*

Even with all that I saw and experienced with my mother, it still did not prepare me for this life change.

That three-year period with my mother only thrusted me into something a teenage child should not have experienced. I was not mentally or emotionally prepared for the experience. However, it was through these experiences I learned the not so good lesson of "masking" my pain. Meaning, it taught me how to hide the abuse, the guilt, the shame, and everything else I had experienced. I became a master hider. This period in my life taught me to never let my outside exterior, reveal my inside wounds. It taught me how to dress it up in nice clothing, how to scent it up with perfume. How to make it up with cosmetics, and how to disguise the many painful and sad times, as happy ones. It was these experiences where I learned the presentation presented, is often predicated on fiction. I learned to present myself and my situation based on the perception of others. In other words, what "you" perceived my life to be, is what I presented. This three-year period taught me how to portray a facade and to do so extremely well! Can anyone relate to this all too common lying game?

To deal with life as a whole and as it was happening, I had to be strong. I had to be prepared mentally, emotionally and spiritually, but I was simply not ready in any of these areas. I was too young in my mind, too immature. Oh, I coped with it all, but coping is not the same as being developed mentally and emotionally to handle the life I was now living with a level of maturity! Both of the practices I learned in how to mask my pain and keep going and to grin and bear it were incredibly unhealthy life styles. By the time I moved to Oakland my spirit was already crushed. This occurred long before my mind could ever reach a healthy maturity level. One where I was not only adjusting and coping, but one where I was appropriately able to process and handle the new lifestyle I had just entered into. For Pete's sake, I had already been through way too much.

My childhood did not yield an opportunity to be mentored, encouraged, enlightened or properly prepared for "real life" let alone one living with a man. This entire situation could have set the course for a much worse outcome, but praise God it did not! You'll see later on in the upcoming chapters. God had his hand upon me, just as he has his hand upon you. Might I remind you of the life of Joseph in the bible. Who could have imagined his life would turn out like it did? God has a purpose and yes, all things do work together for the good of those who love God and are the "called" according to his purpose, (Romans 8:28). Be encouraged as you keep reading.

Talk About A Serious Transition

In a matter of three years and with my new adult life, I've gone from being my mother's keeper, to losing my mother, to meeting my father for the first time, to trying to adjust and reconnect with my childhood, or at the least, settle into my teenage years, to being in an adult relationship, and living with a man. How is that for a serious transition? I'm now living in Oakland, California with a man and working a full-time job at this board and care home. I am seventeen years old and one month away from my eighteenth birthday. I am responsible for cooking meals three times a day, many of which in the beginning, I burned (LOL). I knew how to cook, but just not for seven plus people. I was now grocery shopping monthly with his grandmother, banking, distributing medications to the residents, washing clothes and more. Talk about lifestyle adjustment.

SIDE BAR: *Before I go any further, let me clarify; this is not about the person I moved to Oakland with, nor his family. This is about my experiences from my point of view and the effects on me as a young lady, and as a woman. The young man I moved to Oakland with thirty plus years ago is a wonderful son, husband, father and beloved brother in Christ. He is also my good friend. God is able to make all things new, including me and him! If he did it for us, he can do it for you too! Bless His Name.*

Before long, my new relationship started experiencing some problems. Growing up, I witnessed the women in my circle of influence going through turbulence in their relationships: arguing, fighting, and infidelity. After witnessing such experiences, I determined early on that I would not repeat that lifestyle. Sadly, this is precisely where I found myself.

I was experiencing everything I told myself I would not repeat and with each experience there was much heartache and emotional trauma. This was pain I had never, ever felt or experienced before. How could someone hurt another person like that? I found myself thinking about what my mother must have experienced and I asked myself the question, "how did she survive such pain?" Maybe this is why she drank so much. How do women in general go through this kind of pain and keep going? Why do we repeatedly allow ourselves to suffer? What keeps us returning to painful experiences? Can you believe I have even more questions?

Being that I was not one to keep my mouth shut, I started questioning things that were happening and that just provoked more arguments and more fights. Any relationship riddled with infidelity (although we were not married), arguing and fighting is not a healthy one, for either party. Sometimes, we as women can allow those good times (that are far and few in-between), to convince us we're in a healthy relationship when the truth is we're actually not. We're blinded by the desire of love and the need to feel wanted, so we readily accept the "false representation of love."

SIDE BAR: *An unhealthy relationship does not necessarily mean that either person is a bad person, it could mean that together they're simply not good for one another. If we can be mature enough to face this truth, I believe we can avoid unnecessary pain and potentially harm in the relationships we find ourselves in. Sometimes the level of love required, is the love that realizes you're better apart than you are together and the ability to walk away amicably. That's wise, that's real love and real respect! Also note, being in a relationship, does not constitute a person becoming the property of another. You are not owned by anyone. Women, WE ARE NOT PROPERTY. WE ARE PRECIOUS and WE ARE PRICELESS. Please, KNOW YOUR WORTH!*

NOTE: If you are married, I am not encouraging you to "walk away." In this case, seek prayer and marriage counseling. If you find yourself in a boyfriend or girlfriend type of situation and there are early signs the relationship is unhealthy, please do not continue in this relationship! If you find it difficult to walk away, seek counseling for yourself and gain what's needed to make a healthy choice and if necessary, a safe exit.

The bible tells us in 1 Corinthians 13:4–8 "*Charity suffereth long, and is kind; charity envieth not; charity vaunteth not itself, is not puffed up, doth not behave itself unseemly, seeketh not her own, is not easily provoked, thinketh no evil; rejoiceth not in iniquity, but rejoiceth in the truth; beareth all things, believeth all things, hopeth all things, endureth all things. Charity never faileth: but whether there be prophecies, they shall fail; whether there be tongues, they shall cease; whether there be knowledge, it shall vanish away.*" This scripture tells us how we should measure love, desire love, receive love, give and accept love. Anything else is beneath what God has made available to us

I Was Happy and Excited

With the support of family, we moved into our own place. I was happy and excited and I was looking forward to things changing for the better. After all, moving in together was a sure sign things were looking up, right? Not necessarily true. Unfortunately, our relationship was still facing some very challenging times. By this time, it was early 1985 and I got a job working at a fast food chain. A co-worker I had befriended introduced me to their cousin, who also worked at the facility. The two of us seemed to form an instant friendship. During one of the many fights and subsequent break-ups my boyfriend and I would have, instead of hopping a Greyhound bus and heading back to L.A. as I had been doing regularly, a friend asked her grandmother if I could stay with them temporarily. This ended up being where I would stay when my boyfriend and I fought.

Time to Make a Decision

At this time, I really needed to figure out if I was going to continue in this relationship or finally end it. It was becoming too much and I simply did not want to argue, fight, or go through these experiences any more. I was growing tired. It just seemed so repetitive and I was becoming increasingly scared. When the arguing and fighting first started, I was fighting back. I was not one to be afraid to fight. You hit me, I was going to hit you back! Plus, growing up, I had an uncle who taught me how to box. He was a boxer and he used to teach me boxing techniques and tell me I was not going to fight like a girl. He taught me how to jab, knock a persons' air out of them, put them to sleep with the pinch, where to choke them to cut their air off, how to stand and swing effectively, and how to throw my weight (all ninety-nine pounds) behind a punch. Sadly, I used none of these techniques when we would fight. Go figure.

I was seriously starting to wonder how this relationship would end. Would he seriously hurt me? Would he eventually kill me? Would I hurt or kill him in an effort to protect myself? I really had to consider what I wanted. I am going to be truthful, even going through what I was going through, knowing right over wrong, knowing this was never really going to go anywhere, my heart was involved, and because of that, I stayed for three more years. Am I the only one who chose to stay? Or can anyone else relate?

SIDE BAR: *Your heart can make you choose foolishness over wisdom, danger over safety, and lies over the truth. A person's emotions can make a smart and intellectual person appear unwise. Never judge a woman who is in an unhealthy relationship. Breaking away from matters of the heart can be difficult. Knowing what's right and doing what's right is hard, and those who find themselves in these situations need our support, help, prayers, and for us not to judge or condemn them. They need our under-standing, patience, and unconditional love if they're going to make it out!*

Over the course of time my co-worker and I had become really close. We were really good friends and we could talk about anything. He was very respectful of me and he never once pressured me in any kind of way. He "seemed" to be really shy and he was extremely nice to me. He was funny and instead of causing me pain, he brought joy and laughter to me. It was a very refreshing friendship. We would continue talking over the next two years, during which my tumultuous live-in relationship continued. It wasn't long before he enrolled in the military and left. My sound board, confidant, and joy had left. The beauty is that our friendship was solid then and is solid today. Yes, he and I have remained friends until this day. More on this later. Keep reading.

During my seven-year on-again, off-again relationship, I moved back home to Southern California more times than I care to admit. Only to keep returning to Oakland when in November of 1987, I was shocked, confused, scared and excited to learn I was pregnant. Ever since I was fifteen years old I wanted nothing, but to be pregnant. I wanted this so I could love this child the way I desired to be loved. The way I appeared to have not been loved.

SIDE BAR: *How many of our young girls today set out to get pregnant in an effort to fill a gap in their lives? A gap for love, acceptance and to fit in. How can they give something they themselves have never received? Is this one of the ways they go looking and seeking out love in all the wrong places? Instead of condemning our young girls to hell with our criticism and judgement, let's love them into wholeness with hearts of compassion and understanding. Let's offer them an ear to not only hear, but listen to what may have landed them where they are. Whether they say it or not, our young girls need us, they really do! Let's be there for them!*

I Was in Total Bliss

When I found myself pregnant with a child, I thought, "finally! Someone who will love me for me." I thought that I could right all the wrongs "I perceived" were done to me. I was going to be a good mother and love my child. I was in total bliss. This was all I had been wanting for a long time. After all, most of my teenage friends were already mothers; now I get to join them. I am pregnant!

I was not thinking of the fact that I was in an unhealthy relationship. One where we were facing many challenges. I was not considering how the father of this child felt. Did he want a child? Was he ready for a child? Our situation was clearly the answer for all of these questions; answers I totally dismissed. Was I really ready for a child? The fact that I had not considered the baby itself, was a clear indication I was not ready to be a mother. A mother denies self for the betterment of their child and I knew nothing about this. It was all about me and what I wanted. How sad is this to consider, but oh how real it is! It's a vicious cycle that unfortunately repeats itself, generation after generation. We must endeavor to end it!

My joy of becoming a mother was short-lived. After experiencing some pain in my pelvic area, I caught the bus to a local community hospital where it was discovered that I had an ectopic pregnancy. After being examined, I was informed by the doctor who treated me that if I left the ER that night, there was a great chance I would die. The tube was in jeopardy of bursting. In excruciating pain, I walked to the pay phone down the hall in the ER and called my grandmother collect. I told her what the doctor said and she instructed me to remain in the hospital. I ended up having surgery to remove part of my right tube. I could have never imagined what all of this would lead to.

And Life Takes Yet Another Turn

I asked the doctor where this could have come from and she looked at my file because I had been to this facility before due to an infection and she said "this is a result of your previous infection." I did not know you could have an infection and not have any symptoms. Some of the infections were untreated because I was not aware I was even infected. I was also not aware of the internal damage it could do to a woman. This is what happens when immaturity and inexperience are met with this type of real life situation. Needless to say, I was ashamed, embarrassed and terribly hurt. I thought about the times I had found antibiotics that were being taken without my knowledge. I questioned the occurrences, but chose to deny the truth that was staring me directly in my face.

SIDE BAR: *Sadly, this is yet another all too common scenario. Please, women, young and mature alike, I urge and plead with you to **NOT** have premarital sex. I know, most will think that I am crazy, considering what I am writing in this book. But no, I'm not crazy. It's because of what I am writing in this book that I plead with you to heed my advice and choose not to have premarital sex. Ultimately, the decision is yours and has consequences and repercussions. Whatever decision you make, will yield results. Choose wisely!*

My choice, landed me having surgery with a number of staples across the lower part of my abdomen. Being so young and stupid, I did not consider what all of this could have meant for my future, for my overall health, for my ability of becoming a mother later in life. Choices...I simply had no idea what consequences the future would bring as a result of this experience. This relationship I was in was an on again and off again relationship from 1984 through 1991. So much happened during this time that forced me to grow up even faster than the three years with my mother did, and it taught me so much about "real life."

I was exposed to things and situations that have impacted my life to this very day. I learned about betrayal and the heartache that's associated with an unhealthy relationship. I learned about mental and emotional manipulation and the games people play with the feelings of others. It was during this time I also learned just how strong I was and how much of a fighter I really was. I give all glory to God that I did not end up strung out on drugs, with multiple men in my life, or worst, dead!

SIDE BAR: *There was a grace on my life. The grace of God that brought me through all of this and I believe that* *grace was because God had predestined me to be here at this time, writing this book to share openly, my story. To encourage you the reader, and to offer you the hope I have found in and through Christ Jesus. To let many women know they are NOT alone. To challenge you to not give up, to keep fighting and pushing, even when it may appear you don't have any more fight to give.* **DON'T GIVE UP!** *There is hope in Jesus!*

When You Get Tired, You'll Leave

Prior to one of my last moves home to Southern California, I remember having a telephone conversation with my grandmother. I was calling to inform her that I was on my way back home again. I will never forget her words, she said, "when you get tired, you'll leave" and she was right. In 1988, shortly after going through the ectopic pregnancy experience, I was "truly" tired and I had found myself in a place where enough was really enough. No one had to talk me into leaving this time. No one had to try and get me to see the truth of what I was going through. No one had to force me to leave. I was really ready to leave. The arguments, the fighting and the rest, I was ready for all of it to be over!

My mother's death taught me many things, among them was how to separate, even with pain. Losing her left me with a new motto, a motto that I have carried with me all these years. I have used it to get out of and through some tough situations. That motto is "hurt and move on." With my mind made up, I planned for what I knew would be a hard and painful transition. I was not home in Southern California long before I was asked to return to Oakland, and I did. But this time, I was returning with my own plans. My mind was really made up! With all that I experienced with my mother in southern California, I had no desire to live there anymore. I only returned to Oakland because I had nowhere else to go. I was now thinking with a little clarity, and I was able to devise a plan for my return.

The fog was finally clear; I was finally thinking like I had some sense. My life was no longer being played like a fiddle. I was now making decisions for my own life. How liberating this was for me. This experience had toughened me up and taught me life lessons I would not have otherwise learned. Every experience, good, bad or indifferent will teach us if we're willing to learn. It's all about our perspective. I had learned many great lessons from this period in my life. As my grandmother would say "nothing is better than a bought lesson, and I paid a hefty price for the lessons I learned during this time.

SIDE BAR: *No relationship, regardless of how good or bad it is, is ever easy to separate from. Although hard and difficult to watch, no loved one, be it a friend or family member, will ever be able to convince anyone to leave a relationship until that person is ready to leave. You can talk until you're blue in the face; the individual has to be ready before any change will occur. However, prayer is always in order and the fervent and effectual prayers of the righteous will availeth much. If you know someone in an unhealthy relationship, pray for them and trust God. Be there to support, to listen and to gently encourage. But remember, the choice will always be theirs to make.*

Key Points:

- Have you ever tried to run from your shadow? If so, what happens? It follows you, right? When I was trying to get away. I needed a break and a change to be free from all of the pain I had experienced. I never considered that running was not going to produce anything new other than a new location. I never considered I would still be the same person, with the same pain, the same viewpoints and the same mind set, just in a different location.

- Changing locations does not necessarily change a person. I imagine there are plenty of young women who are running from something in life and they think a new man, a new baby, a new job or new house will change the internal person, it won't. The change must first take place on the inside. Real change happens from the inside out, and not from the outside in.

- I was a young girl who was excited about "my fantasy" and my fantasy was just that—a fantasy.

I, like many other girls, fantasized about having a husband, kids, and a big white house with a picket fence. Isn't this what most girls fantasize about? The dream most of us were sold, right along with the doll house we received for Christmas? Unfortunately, I learned there is a difference between our fantasies, our dreams and our truth. I also learned a young girl's fantasy, if not addressed and refocused, can later become her nightmare as a grown woman.

- It's okay and even healthy to dream. Our dreams provide ammunition for us to work towards fulfilling our dreams and allows us to look forward to celebrating with a great sense of accomplishment! So yes, dare to dream the dream God has placed in your heart and move with him to fulfill it.

Questions:

1. How and when do we prepare our daughters and young girls for the real world?

2. When, if ever, is it a good time for parents, mentors, and encouragers to step back?

3. Is more discussion necessary to facilitate healthier, platonic relationships between young girls and women? If so, how and where do we begin these discussions?

4. Is teen pregnancy a problem? If so, why and what can we do about the problem? Especially in this day and time we now live in?

5. How do we ensure our daughters and young women know their worth?

6. Why are we not talking about "premarital sex?"

7. How do we bring the discussion of Domestic Violence to the forefront? Especially in those seemingly untouched arenas.

Prayer:

Father I come praying for the young girl or young woman who may have found themselves pregnant and don't know which way to turn or where to go for help.

I pray for clarity of mind Father God. I pray you would grant them wisdom to know what to do. You said in your word in James 1:5 *"If any of you lack wisdom, let him ask of God, that giveth to all men liberally, and upbraideth not; and it shall be given him."* I pray you would grant them knowledge, courage and the strength to make wise decisions for them and their unborn child. Grant them the courage to not buckle under pressure or cave in to fear. Place around them women of wisdom, to gird and to help navigate them through this life change. Your word declares in Proverbs 11:14, *"Where no counsel is, the people fall: but in the multitude of counsellors there is safety."* You did not give us a spirit of fear Father, according to 2 Timothy 1:7, *"For God hath not given us the spirit of fear; but of power, and of love, and of a sound mind."* Close the mouths of the nay-sayers, silence the torment of the enemy and grant them the ability to hear you and move obediently with your spirit. Your word says in Isaiah 30:21 *"And thine ears shall hear a word behind thee, saying, "This is the way, walk ye in it, when ye turn to the right hand, and when ye turn to the left."* Help them to see the blessings they behold according to your word in Psalms 127:3 *"Lo, children are a heritage of the Lord: and the fruit of the womb is his reward."* Father God, help those who are with child to do as Hannah did, Lord and dedicate their children to you, and just like you did with Samuel, you will do with their children, bless them and use them abundantly. 1 Samuel 1:28, *"Therefore also I have lent him to the Lord; as long as he liveth he shall be lent to the Lord. And he worshipped the Lord there."* We thank you, Father God and we pray this prayer in the awesome and powerful name of our Lord and Savior, Jesus the Christ, Amen!

My Lord and God, I am in an unhealthy relationship, Lord. I pray you would give me peace, the peace you said in Philippians 4:7, *"And the peace of God, which passeth all understanding, shall keep your hearts and minds through Christ Jesus."* I pray for the peace to hear you and to know the direction in which you desire me to go according to your word in Isaiah 30:21, which says, *"And thine ears shall hear a word behind thee, saying, "This is the way, walk ye in it, when ye turn to the right hand,*

and when ye turn to the left." I pray you would send your angels to protect me and to keep me and my children safe from evil and harm's way. Lord, I ask you to give me the courage to leave when the time is right, grant me what I need to wait until then according to your word in Psalms 27:14 *"Wait on the LORD: be of good courage, and he shall strengthen thine heart: wait, I say, on the LORD."* I pray you would open wide the door for me to escape, Father and that you would send me the help and support I need to transition to a place of safety. Father you said in your word that I can have the confidence of knowing if I ask anything according to your will, you would hear me, as it is written in 1 John 5:14, *"And this is the confidence that we have in him, that, if we ask any thing according to his will, he heareth us."* I know it's not your will for any of your precious daughters to be in unhealthy relationships or to be hurt on any level. Therefore, I believe this prayer will yield forth a harvest of safe transition and a newness of life for me, because I ask in that name that is above every name and you promised in John 14:13 *"And whatsoever ye shall ask in my name, that will I do, that the Father may be glorified in the Son."* May the Father be glorified in my life and in each of your daughters' lives, that we all may find life and live it more abundantly. In Jesus' Name I pray! Amen.

Chapter 6

"Making it Through the Discovery Phase"

"Behold, what manner of love the Father hath bestowed
upon us, that we should be called the sons of God:
therefore the world knoweth us not, because it knew
him not. Beloved, now are we the sons of God, and it
doth not yet appear what we shall be: but we know
that, when he shall appear, we shall be like him; for we
shall see him as he is."

1 John 3:1–2

Faced with a Choice

With a clear head I told my grandmother I was returning to Oakland and that I was going to get my own place this time. With this conversation, I returned to Oakland with a different outlook and a different perspective. The drive to leave the relationship and to get my own place only gained strength when my little brother needed my help. After a conversation with my boyfriend, I knew he was not ready to be a father and I understood this. The truth is we were both young and knew absolutely nothing about being guardians, let alone parents. Nevertheless, I was now faced with a choice of taking care of my brother or to continue to live as I was and do my own thing.

I was probably going to have to work two jobs to survive and how would I do this and care for my fourteen-year-old brother. Now, I was really going to have to consider my life's options and what I was going to do. I had to seriously consider my life choices, my goals and my future, as well as his. He needed my help and I was not sure I would be able to provide him with the help he needed? Could I, as a young woman myself, provide this young boy with the care, support, guidance and stability he needed to have a chance at a successful life? This young boy who only six years earlier had lost his mother? Was I capable of dealing with his issues of losing his mother. Was I capable of helping him to adjust? Heck, had I properly adjusted myself? Trust me, these may have been the questions I was faced with then, but I can assure you today that I was not thinking as clearly about them then as I am today in hindsight.

SIDE BAR: I draw attention to this here to say to those who are faced with caring for a younger relative, be it your sibling's or other relatives? Please think carefully and plan appropriately. It is never wrong to offer help and support to family who need you, especially a young child. But if you're young yourself, certainly seek the wise counsel of someone older, more experienced with life and successful parenting that can offer you the support you need. Taking on a child, or children is and will be a huge undertaking. Don't go it alone, if you don't have to! There are resources available to you. Contact the Social or Family Services Agency in your area and seek the help and support of other counseling if needed. Please, take advantage of the support available to you. **See Links/ websites to government agencies under "Resources" at the end of this chapter.**

Well, shortly before learning my brother needed my help, I had a dream about my mother and in the dream she told me to take care of my siblings, actually she told me to keep us together. With this information I determined that she was confirming my decision to take care of my little brother, so that's what I did. With my decision made, I proceeded to get a second job at a new home improvement store opening up in the area. I started looking for an apartment close to where I would be working the second job and wouldn't you know it, I found an apartment just a few blocks away. I started buying items for my new apartment and stacking them in the closet I shared with my boyfriend. A few months later, after saving up enough money, I moved out into my own place.

SIDE BAR: *If you're a woman and you find yourself considering to leave a relationship that may have been troubled, seek counsel in doing so. The counsel can be with a relative, a friend, or a professional, so long as it's a trusted resource. If it's needed, please do so. Now a day it can be dangerous to separate from an intimate relationship. There are many safe houses you can go to if you feel the person you're leaving is a serious threat to your well-being, and to that of your children, if you have children. We've all had to take precautions when leaving relationships, it is nothing to be embarrassed by. Be wise and contemplative when considering your transition if danger lurks, and the less people who know, the better. Take a look at the resources in the back of this book to find an agency who can assist you, if needed.*

I Had No Clue

I was now in my early twenties and for the first time, living in my own place just me and my fourteen-year-old brother I was now raising. I was working two jobs to ensure I could keep a roof over our heads and make sure he had everything he needed. Here I am faced with yet another shift or turn in my life. I had no clue as to how to raise a fourteen-year-old boy. I knew nothing about raising a child period. I mean I babysat all of my cousins and sister and brother, but raising a kid . . . I had not a clue.

I had to register him in school, make sure he had school supplies and clothes, etc. I now had first-hand experience of what my mother was experiencing, only she had four children. I was now thinking about things other than myself. I was thinking about him, taking everything I learned from my experience with my mother and trying to do differently. I made every attempt to be there when he needed me, be present at school, on projects, help with assignments and homework. I made sure he had food and lunch money, etc. The stress alone from having to miss work to attend school meetings was more than I anticipated and how that trickled down to being short on bills was an altogether new experience. These are all things he knew nothing about. Even at fourteen-years old, he wanted to help, even though he didn't know the depth of what was going on. Children can sense when things are not right. Yes, they really can.

Although this experience was not long term, it was long enough for me to relate to being a parent and having to worry about another life; providing for someone other than myself. I learned a lot with this experience and doing so while still trying to still discover who I was. However, looking back now, I would not change a thing. I have no regrets for caring for my brother. It taught me a great deal. As I said early, there is no better teacher of life, than life itself!

It wasn't long before my little brother was involved in some activity at school with other kids and because he was let's say "different" and much taller than some of the other kids, he was the one who found himself in juvenile hall as a result. I was devastated and I did not know what to do. By nature, I am a fighter, so I thought "I am going to fight this" and I did. I reached out to lawyers, those in the juvenile system, and Oprah. Yes, I reached out to Oprah Winfrey. I was young, hopeful, and did not know any better. It turned out to be a representative from a local chapter of a well-known African American agency who came to our rescue. I thought my brother was being unfairly accused and I reached out to everyone I could to get the help we needed. This entire experience cost me a couple of jobs, but he was my brother and he was worth it to me!

After this whole ordeal was over and my brother was released, I decided I needed help raising him and made the decision to return home where my grandmother and aunts could assist me with my little brother. I figured it would be best for the both us to be back home near family. We loaded up my little Isuzu I-mark with all of our belongings and with $80 in my purse, we hit I-5 headed back to Southern California. I was home for a short period of time before I felt the pull to return to Oakland. This time when I returned to Oakland it was not by request, but by my own desire to return and make Oakland my home. I had been in Oakland long enough to be comfortable. I had established my own friendships and relationships and I felt confident enough I could survive on my own.

Here We Go Again

I told my grandmother I was returning to Oakland for the last time. Sound familiar? I told her I would get a job and my own place again. This time when I returned I stayed with a couple of friends off and on for a little while before moving in with another friend and sleeping on their floor in the corner of their living room, while I dressed out of my trunk. I only mention this because I was told I could not sleep on their couch, or love seat . . . it still astonishes me to this day. I later moved in with my ex-boyfriend's mother who had relocated to Oakland. This is the lady I was living with at the time of my mother's death. She was then and is to this day like a mother to me.

By this time, it's November of 1991 and I was hired to work the night shift for a national food distribution com-pany. It's my first job working the graveyard shift and

I stroll in, meet my co-worker and we hit it off immediately. We are the only two women working among a warehouse full of men and we quickly become best friends. After a while of working at this company I can feel myself beginning to laugh and feel happy again. I was beginning to feel even more free than I had been.

I have made a decision to reinvent myself and why not? There had always seemed to be this pull on the inside of me for something better and I wanted it. I never believed the life I had been living was truly the life I was meant to live. I just never understood how to break the shackles that seemed to have been holding me there. I always had this feeling of being dissatisfied and unfulfilled, with a gaping void in my life. It felt like I was merely existing, but not wholeheartedly living. It was like being forced to where a pair of shoes that were clearly not my size. Can you imagine walking all day in a pair of shoes that did not fit? If so, then you understand how very uncomfortable I was in this place.

SIDE BAR: *There are a lot more people than many of us may know who feel as though they are different. Granted, we are all different and that's a part of the beauty of God's creative genius. However, when I say different I don't mean better, I simply mean different. We all have unique and specific purposes for which we were created. That's how the body of Christ was designed to function and work together. The head can't do what the foot does, or vice, versa.*

If a person does not know who they are or why they were created, that can pave a path for a very lonely and frustrating journey. And sadly, there are those who don't know who they are, or why they were created. There are those who are afraid to even admit they have this issue, this question, or are on this quest. They fear they will be misunderstood, or judged as I was. I was accused of thinking I was better than others, when what I was simply trying to figure out was who I was? Why I was created? What my purpose was for being here? Perhaps, many don't ask this question and so it may seem, shall we say, uncommon.

It's unfortunate, but we tend to cast off those who are, or may function differently than we do and most times, it's these same people who shoot up schools, jump off bridges, hang themselves, or turn to drugs, or other forms of self-medicating. Because I sometimes felt alone, even though I was almost always surrounded by others, I was considering suicide and no one knew. All because the search for answers were sometimes unbearable and lonely for me. We all know someone who was different or was an introvert, or they were just assumed to be "strange." Just because a person does not function the way others do, does not mean their weak, strange, or weird for that matter; it just means they are beautifully unique. We should desire and learn how to be more accepting of the difference in qualities and abilities we as a people have and learn to appreciate the beauty of being unique. It would make for a better world.

This new phase in my life was my discovery phase. For the first time, I am trying to discover who I am. What type of life do I want to live? What do I want to do with my life? For a period of time all I knew was to be my mother's keeper and protector. The one who looked after my siblings when they were with us. The one who was keeping secrets and trying to cover up everything that was wrong with my life. And now, I actually get to live my own life! It feels like some sort of weird rebirth, and it feels good! I have found my independence and therefore, I am not dependent upon anyone for anything and that feels incredibly liberating. Being independent is something my grandmother had always taught me to be and now, I was actually doing it and living it. If felt great!

I no longer have someone trying to make me conform to their way of thinking, doing and living. I am my own person, a working class citizen with a checking and savings account and I have credit! I thought to myself, this is the American dream! Now, I really feel like I am on the path to the life I was always destined to live and it feels amazing to me. For years I felt as though I had been in a place of bondage; enslaved to a life of hell. I was now footloose and fancy free in this new discovery phase of my life and I was glad about it! Having my own income, the liberty to do as I pleased and a comfortable living Condition, void of tension and discomfort. It was great!

Oh No She Didn't . . . Yes, I DID!

I was having fun hanging out with my coworkers. After work we would meet up at bar near the job, yes, I said bar. We would go there to shoot darts and unwind. I have never liked the taste of alcohol so when I would drink, it was usually a sweet drink like a fuzzy navel, which I would drink through a straw because I did not like the taste of the alcohol. Yes, after everything I experienced with my mother, I did drink and yes, it would remind me of how I hated it, but I would still do it. On occasion, I even found myself tipsy. It was a feeling I did not like but I still continued to drink! Can anyone relate to doing things they did not necessarily like, or am I the only one? The bible states the following in. *Romans 7:15–20 "For that which I do I allow not: for what I would, that do I not; but what I hate, that do I. If then I do that which I would not, I consent unto the law that it is good.*

Now then it is no more I that do it, but sin that dwelleth in me. For I know that in me (that is, in my flesh,) dwelleth no good thing: for to will is present with me; but how to perform that which is good I find not. For the good that I would I do not: but the evil which I would not, that I do. Now if I do that I would not, it is no more I that do it, but sin that dwelleth in me."

During this time, I was also smoking weed. I did not like the smell of the weed on me, so when I finished smoking I would brush my teeth, spray perfume on me, wash my hands and put lotion on to mask the scent. One of my older cousins introduced me to weed when I was younger. After this initial bad experience that left me sick to my stomach and after drinking lots of milk because I could not handle it, I did not smoke again until the last two years of my mother's life. After her death, I quit for a year or so, and I started smoking again shortly after moving to Oakland.

Side Bar: *You might be asking why I am sharing this and why it's relevant. Here's why, it's relevant! Pretty much* everybody has smoked marijuana and pretty much every-body drinks, socially, or otherwise. Most people who have a "so-called" status, won't tell you, or don't want anyone to know they have smoked marijuana, or done other stuff before. Can I tell you, this is the stuff we should be sharing with people? This is the stuff they want to know. It's not that most people want to know your business and let's not be ignorant, there are those who do want to know your stuff to throw stones at you, but there are those who genuinely want to know for reasons of encouragement! They don't just want to know; they NEED to know.

Perhaps someone has an addiction to marijuana, drinking, or another addiction or condition. We, those of us in the pulpit or on the stage, make it HARD for people to relate to us because we appear unreal to them. We make life with Jesus unrealistic! We leave them believing we walk on water and that we have not done anything, never experienced anything, or done anything stupid before. Believe me, I have done some stuff, everybody has! But, we are NOT what we've done. It is NOT who we are! Share your struggles, because in doing so, you *are sharing your victories and people need to know by example the victory that is available in and through Christ Jesus! We need to let people know while this walk may be difficult sometimes, it's not impossible. Be an example of God's awesome power and his ability to deliver and make you free!*

I was in discovery mode and weed smoking and drinking was what I did! It was the life and the environment I had come from. I have never liked the thought of anything having control over me so I would eventually stop doing both. Plus, there was this nagging pull that was on the inside of me and periodically it messed up my good times, if you know what I am saying. I felt like I was being pulled in two different directions; one was the environment I had come from and was currently in, and the other that was pulling me is what I knew was my future, and my destiny. But the two were total opposites of each other. How do I release the one that I know is my past and no good for me, to attain the one I knew was on the inside of me? The one that was my future and my destiny? This is a quest I would be on for a while.

Being Different Is Not a Popular Trend

I was always a little different than most and I tried to fit in and be a part of the crowd. It was my perception you know; I didn't see things as everyone else may have seen. I know, everyone is not supposed to think alike and I get that. It's just that my thought process to me was always different. I didn't see the glass half empty, or half full for that matter. What I would see would have many of you scratching your heads, so I will leave that discussion for another time. I have always been a deep thinker, and that sometimes made it difficult for me to fit in. I had friends, and we hung out together and we did what friends would normally do. However, for me, those moments still seemed a little different for me and sometimes made me feel a little lonely. I know, how is this possible? Trust me, it is. Can anyone else relate?

You are supposed to be able to tell your friends how you're feeling and what's going on in your life, right? Well, I would have moments where I wanted to tell them the things I was experiencing, but how do you tell someone what you yourself don't understand? What you are still trying to figure out? I seemed to have a mind of an older person and this made it difficult for me to relate sometimes. I was too serious. It's hard to explain. I was just different. When hanging out with my friends, I would always have these questions in the back of my mind; like why am I doing this, that or the other? There would literally be a separate conversation going on in my mind. Back then it was crazy, but today it makes total sense.

It's weird you know, when I would return home from being out with my friends, I would find myself reviewing and analyzing the events of the day, evaluating the entire situation. I know, it's strange. All of these things (what would be considered to be fun stuff by most) were just things I was doing, but they never felt right. Most times I felt like a fish out of water, but I never said anything to anyone. I'm sure I was a total buzz kill on many occasions. Who could I tell what I was experiencing? If I did mention it to some of my friends, coworkers, or loved ones, they would have, no doubt, thought that I was strange. Perhaps some of you reading this book right now think I am crazy.

SIDE BAR: *I wonder how many people, be it teenagers, young adults, or mature adults who may be feeling the pressure of doing things that go against everything on the inside of them. I mean you do it, but it's not who you are, or what you do. You just go along with it, pretending to enjoy what you're doing, or you may even enjoy what you're doing, but you know it's not you. You just want to be with the in crowd. You feel like it's what's necessary for you to get to where you're going, or to attain the friends and the status you want. Let me assure you, it's not going to yield the return you might think it is! Be true to who you are and dare to be different, to be unique, dare to be your true "authentic" self! Trust me, there will be NO REGRETS for being who God created you to be!*

Sadly, many people are experiencing bouts of identity crisis just as I was, and it has nothing to do with what their sir name is? Feeling the pressure of making a bold and often times critical decision to stand alone can be quite terrifying and accepting the fact that you're different can be pressure all in itself. Especially in a world where there is enormous pressure to do as everyone else does. Think about it this way, when we think about launching a business, we research to see what the trend is, in other words, what everybody else is doing. We get on various social media sites because that's the trend. What if when considering to launch your new business, you said I am going to market my business, but I am not going to use social media. Most people would be like, what? You can't do that. What if God told you he was going to make you successful, but you had to do it his way and he instructed you not to use social media. You would be like, what? That's not going to work!

My point is this, most people today buckle to the pressure of yielding to what's trending, what's popular, what everyone else is doing. They justify their fear by saying things like "It's what everyone else is doing." You have many people in positions now who can take a stand, but won't out of fear of what it will cost them. Dr. Martin Luther King, Jr. dared to be different and made a difference. Rosa Parks dared to be different and made a difference. Mother Teresa dared to be different and made a difference. Malcom X dared to be different and made a difference. Jesus dared to be different and made a difference in all of our lives. Each of us possess a unique set of characteristics, talents, abilities, gifts, and a purpose that sets us apart from the next person. Consider this fact, no one person has the same set of fingerprints. Will you choose to be true to who you are, even if it means taking a stand, and even if it's not popular to do so? Will the real, true, and authentic you please STAND UP?

SIDE BAR: *Outside of God, you will never really know who you are and what your purpose is. Many people go through this life without ever really discovering their true identity. Most will live unfulfilled lives, or find themselves forever searching, but doing so in all the wrong places and* *in doing all the wrong things and even in being in a relationship with the wrong person. The truth of who you are is only found in the one who created you and that's God! If you're at a period in your life where you do not know who you are, go to God. With him, you will learn who you are and you can then allow his grace and the power of his Holy Spirit to help you to be your true authentic self. Don't let the pressure of others make you conform to someone, or something you're not. It takes courage to stand alone and more often than not when you dare to be different, you will be standing alone. Be encouraged, God will always be with you. If God be for you, who can be against you!*

I Am Finally Beginning to See Some Light

Life would go on; the discovery phase was in full motion. I am still employed at my night job, I have a new car and a place to call my own which, I share with a roommate. I am finally beginning to see some light and my future is looking extremely bright to me. I am able to smile and enjoy myself more and more. I am truly discovering who Ceola is and life is getting better and sweeter And just when I thought it could not get any better, or any sweeter, while working the night shift, I met the man who would become my first husband. We'll read more about my first marriage in a couple of pages, and yes, I said my first marriage. Keep reading.

Working on this job would bring with it many life changes and some new relationships and one such relationship was with a man by the name of James Rodriguez (Kimo). For whatever reason, Kimo grabbed a hold of me spiritually and would not let me go. He became my first "spiritual Father" I know that now. Every day Kimo would invite me to sit with him by his locker and he would be pulling out all kinds of Max Lucado pamphlets and books and cassette tapes by Pat Robertson from the 700 Club to share with me. He would tell me stories that would make me think, you know. He would tell me how much Jesus loved me, but he never once made me feel like I was being pressured into a belief system. I felt like he was sharing a love story that I wanted to be a part of.

I felt drawn to this love he talked about. It made me curious to know more. I had known about Jesus and God all my life, but it had never been shared with me by someone who had such a love for God and you could feel it when Kimo spoke. I mean my grandmother shared God with me and she encouraged me to always believe and trust in God and I knew she loved God, but it was different. She taught me to always pray and to pray about everything. But the way Kimo talked about God made me believe you could get to know this God on a much more intimate level. His conversations made me hunger for more of this God he shared with me. The entire time I was employed at this job, Kimo poured into me. I know all of this was divinely orchestrated by God and not one-word God allowed him to plant in me would die. These conversations with Kimo helped me a great deal and yes, I read the material and I listened to the cassette tapes he gave me and believe it, or not, I still have the things he gave to me all those years ago.

SIDE BAR: *I remember talking with a friend of mine and they had been in "church" all their lives and I remember I shared with them they needed to have a "relationship" with God and I remember the pause on the phone and their response "I've been in church all my life and no one ever told me I needed to have a relationship with God." I was floored by this response. It made me think and inquire of God 1) how many more people were occupying the pews of our church buildings who did not have a relationship with God and 2) how many people even KNOW that we should have relationship with God, or even that such a thing was available, desired of God, encouraged by God through the very bible we say we read, or that it is what we were created for?*

Along the path of life God has people who are strategically positioned at specific times to do a specific task to help us arrive at his will for our lives. However, we must be willing and obedient to not only acknowledge those moments, but be willing to follow the course. You may be thinking how will I know when those moments arrive? Trust me, if you're seeking God, thirsting after him, you will know. God promises us in his word in Proverbs 8:17 "I love them that love me; and those that seek me early shall find me." Are you seeking God?

Another Dream

Sometime after starting my new job, I would have another dream. I had not dreamt a lot since dreaming of my mother telling me to keep my siblings together. However, this particular dream I have never shared with anyone. The night my ex-boyfriend's grandmother passed away, my phone rang and it was her. She said "Ceola, this is (her name), I was calling to tell you bye." Just about that time my phone rang and it woke me up from sleeping and it was my ex-boyfriend calling to tell me his grandmother had a heart-attack and the ambulance was taking her to the hospital. He told me what hospital they were taking her to and it was the hospital less than ten minutes from where I lived at the time. By the time I got there, she had passed away. I was shocked by her death, but more so by the dream I had just minutes before she passed, the dream his call had just awakened me from.

The dreams and visions were not as frequent from 1983 through 1989. Now in my mid-twenties, the dreams were starting up again. I was not in church at this time and I was being tormented constantly by a spirit of fear. I was so tormented by this spirit that I actually believed what I was being told and that was, that I was going to die. I was having all kinds of nightmares almost every night. No one knew that I would keep Nyquil to help me sleep through the night. I didn't like the taste of alcohol, so I would whisk down the Nyquil quickly to sleep through the nights. I thought it would help me with the tormenting spirit of fear, but I was wrong.

SIDE BAR: *You can't deal with a spiritual issue in a natural way. Ponder on this a while.*

The torment continued and became so heavy that I had actually considered suicide. A secret I kept from my new boyfriend and from those closest to me. Imagine this, we were always around people at family gatherings, at events and no one knew what I was dealing with, what I was considering. I was fine during the day and no tormenting spirit, so long as I was around other people. I was no longer working the night shift, so it was at night when my boyfriend went to work that I suffered with the torment of fear. This occurred all through my mid-twenties and I never shared this with anyone. How I maintained jobs and functioned as normally as I did could only be by the grace of God!

SIDE BAR: *My passion for supporting, encouraging and uniting women is because I know first-hand the torment some of us go through and how some of us suffer in silence. Even those of us who look normal, function normal, dress normal, talk normal, conduct business normal, etc. How many "normal" people have you known that have committed suicide and left those behind scratching their heads because "we never knew anything was wrong." Why is that? Are we as a people so "self-consumed" with* *our own issues of life, that we can't see, or don't want to see what's going on in the lives of others?*

NOTE: No one can tell me God is not real, that he does not love us and watch over us. I know first-hand because I know what I have been through. What God has brought me through. If I were not assured God placed in my heart to write this book, to tell my story, very personal and intimate details about my life, no one would be the wiser. But I know God will receive all the glory, so I write with great expectation and joy in my heart knowing many will be victorious and overcome!

Now, I am sure there will be many who will think back and say, there is no way she was dealing with all of what she has written in this book; how could she have been? She "appeared" to be normal. She was not seeing a psychiatrist. She was not crying all the time. She was not complaining. She did not seem crazy. She was laughing and hanging out with people and doing

everything everybody else was. How? I will tell you how
. . . The Blood of Jesus! I know my redeemer LIVES!

I would continue to suffer with the spirit of torment
until 1994. It was around this same time when I was
invited by my ex-boyfriend (yes, this would be the one I
moved to Oakland with eleven years earlier) to listen to a
Pastor on the radio out of Atlanta, Georgia, his name was
Dr. Charles Stanley. My ex would also invite me to attend
a church he was attending in Oakland. I agreed to go
and visit the church and learned it was the same church
a really good friend of mine's family was attending and
so I began visiting on a regular basis. After visiting this
church for a while, I would eventually join and get bap-
tized again. I continued attending this church for a few
years and the tormenting spirit left, only to return some
years later at my invitation. I'll explain in later chapters.
Keep reading.

Key Points:

- Sharing is caring and it's okay to share your story, actually it's liberating and I encourage you to do so. The bible tells us there is victory in sharing or testimony Revelations 12:11 *"And they overcame him by the blood of the Lamb, and by the word of their testimony; and they loved not their lives unto the death."* Don't deny your passion out of fear of persecution. I am so passionate about sharing my story and educating women and doing so openly. Because I did not have anyone to help me, I am very determined in helping other women avoid unnecessary pitfalls and painful experiences, if at all possible. I will speak to all who will listen!

- Fear is a form of bondage and if allowed; fear will render you powerless and you become enslaved to it. Don't be afraid to accept what God has said about you, who he has called you to be, or of what your purpose is. You've been called by the Only Wise God, honor him and accept your calling.

- In all honestly, you know when God has chosen you. He will not only tell you, but God being a loving Father, will always send those who will call out your gift, calling or your anointing. When he does, the bold attacks of the enemy soon ensue. I did not know I had a prophetic call or mantle on my life. I did not know I was a threat and a target of the enemy? I did not know I had a purpose and I surely was not aware of the significance of that purpose. We must listen and truly be in tune spiritually!

- Your story is not an isolated story. If not told, it's a missed opportunity for you to empower another, to encourage another, to inspire another, to motivate another, to shed light with another sister. I know we haven't told you, but your story is a story we are sitting on the edge of our seats waiting to hear. You know why, because we're waiting excitedly to hear your triumphs, your victories, your success stories and your God-given power to overcome! Transparency builds trust and we have to be willing the bear the cross and tell our testimonies and do so openly and wisely. I've discovered in talking transparently with many women over the years that this is not just my story. It's the story of many, many women who are afraid to share their story out of fear of being judged and frowned upon. The more we women trust God and open up, the more united, the more powerful, the more triumphant and the more victorious we will be. And the many more women we will see overcome. Glory to God! So go ahead girl and proclaim your power in overcoming. Break those shackles!

• Do you know when you are triumphant with God what that means? I mean if we're willing to endure and come through the periods of testing. I am a firm believer that we live so others may live. In other words, I believe our experiences more often than not, are not only lessons for us, but also for the benefit of others. Because of what God allowed in my life and what he alone has brought me through; I am now able to share my test and testimony openly via this book. A book I know beyond the shadow of a doubt God will use to encourage and help many. Not because of me, but because the God who did it for me is the same God who will also do it for you and many others. Take note!

- Wise choices bring forth better outcomes. Be not dismayed if the choices you're required to make are difficult, find the courage to make them and do so wisely. Even seeking counsel if necessary. Part of being a mature adult, is being able to make mature life altering decisions and wisely doing so! Yes, use wisdom!

- There is no better teacher than life itself and every experience births knowledge if we're willing to view the experiences as an opportunity for both learning and growing.

- Be careful of the "discovery phases" in your life. This phase is like walking a tight rope. In order to avoid danger, you have to be well balanced. I had just come through another very tumultuous period in my life where I was enjoying my "liberty." However, living your life without structure, discipline, integrity and some degree of values and morals can be deadly. Use caution if and when in this phase.

- Understand, there are traps the enemy sets for you, but God will protect his own, even when we don't recognize his protection until later in life. These traps can be pivotal moments and often are life altering.

Resources

1. Here's the link to an interesting article by Ramona W. Denby and Jessica Ayala School of Social Work, University of Nevada Las Vegas, Las Vegas, Nevada, USA— http://parented.wdfiles. com/local—files/siblings/Adult%20Siblings%20 Raising%20Younger%20Siblings.pdf

2. Administration for Children and Families—You can find more information on their website at http://www.acf.hhs.gov/

3. Child and Family Services Review—You can find more information on their website at http://www.acf.hhs.gov/

4. Children's Bureau—You can find out more information on their website at http://www.acf.hhs.gov/programs/cb

Questions:

1. Are you faced with an identity crisis or found yourself questioning your existence? Who you are? Why you are here? What you're to do? If so, this is an excellent place to be. The quest is always initiated by God, it's a form of wooing you by the Father. It's a way he gently nudges you to begin to seek him so you may find him, to knock so he can open the door for you and to ask of him, so

he can give to you. This is a great place to be. Be open and enjoy the journey.

2. Can you recall a time in your life where God strategically placed someone in your life (like my Kimo) who poured into you and where that experience was pivotal in your life?

3. If so, I would like you to think about that time; what was happening in your life? How did this experience shift your life? Kind of like the GPS in your car, redirecting you to avert a delay, an accident, or prevent you from getting off course. Reflect on this moment asking God to bring it fully to your memory and journal it as he gives it to you. I guarantee you, it will be a powerful experience!

4. Can you look back over your life and see where different choices would have yielded a different outcome? What did you learn from this experience and how has it helped you in where you are in your life now?

5. Have you ever made the sacrifice to care for a child, or other relative? If so, what was the result? If not,

would you consider it and how would you prepare for the transition?

Prayer:

Father God I come before you thanking you for how perfectly you love and protect me. How you have provided everything I could ever need. I thank you that you have not left me without wisdom for you word declares in James 1:5, *"If any of you lack wisdom, let him ask of God, that giveth to all men liberally, and upbraideth not; and it shall be given him."* I thank you Lord that you have so strategically ordered my steps and that your word declares the steps of a good man are order by the Lord, according to Psalm 37:23. "I thank you for the difficult times that you have so graciously brought me through with your wonderful grace and unlimited compassion, as written in Romans 9:15 *"For he saith to Moses, I will have mercy on whom I will have mercy, and I will have compassion on whom I will have compassion."* Lord, thank you for keeping me safe from all evil and harm's way.

Father, I also come seeking clarity to know who I am in you, my identity and your will and purpose for my life. For you word declares in Ephesians 2:10 *"For we are his workmanship, created in Christ Jesus unto good works, which God hath before ordained that we should walk in them."* Show me my children's purposes with you and help me to stand firm on your word that you have given us all things that pertain unto life and godliness per your word in 2 Peter 1:3–4 *"According as his divine power hath given unto us all things that pertain unto life and godliness, through the knowledge of him that hath called us to glory and virtue: whereby are given unto us exceeding great and precious promises: that by these ye might be partakers of the divine nature, having escaped the corruption that is in the world through lust."* I earnestly pray for your will to be done in my life and in the lives of my children and that through our lives, you would be glorified. I pray this prayer in Jesus Holy Name, Amen!

Chapter 7

"A Ten Year Journey"

"Therefore, if any man be in Christ, he is a new creature: old things are passed away; behold, all things are become new."

2 Corinthians 5:17

To Be Married, To Have Children or Not?

Working the night shift at my job I would meet the man who would later become my first husband and there was something interesting and different about him. This man had no shame and that was a quality I liked about him a lot. He made no secrets about how he felt about me and this was a switch from what I had previously experienced. He would leave flowers and love notes on my desk. He knew I loved plants and fresh flowers and he would be in cahoots with my coworker to sneak the keys to my car so he could leave plants and flowers there for me. He would leave cards all over my office for me and he did not care what our coworkers thought. They would tease him and make fun of him and he just didn't care. He was absolutely adorable to me, and an all-around good guy.

We "officially" began dating some months after I started working the night shift. Together, we would have a really wonderful time and relationship. We had given each other nicknames in the beginning of our relationship and these would be the names we would continue to call each other for the duration of our nineteen-year relationship. So much so that at our wedding ceremony when the pastor asked us to recite our vows, we addressed each other by our nicknames and not our birth names. Our guests chuckled at this.

By this time in my life, I was sure I had finally figured it out. I was sure I knew who I was and what I wanted for my life. I was sure I wanted the life that was being presented to me in this relationship. The life I was now living with him, the life that was a blast on all levels! We were doing lots of stuff together and we were inseparable. When you saw him, you saw me, and it was just the way he wanted it, and because he wanted it, he made me want it, too.

In the latter part of 1992, I was hired in my first executive assistant position and life couldn't be better! We moved into this big beautiful three bedroom, two bath home. I had finally found home and for the first time, I understood that a home was more than an address. Being in my own home now, I was able to decorate my new home exactly the way I wanted it. Since a child I've always had an eye for decorating, for beautifying my surroundings, for the blending of colors and the selecting and placement of furnishings and I was able to be free and creative in my own home. For some, this may seem small, but to me it was a major statement and accomplishment. It even felt more like home because we were so in love and so happy. A year earlier, before we moved in together he bought me a Rottweiler; a dog I did not want. We named the pup "Titan Von" and he carried his last name. We had official papers on him and had to register him, etc. Titan became the dog I could not be without. For the next two years we would host family gatherings and BBQ's at our home. His parents, siblings, cousins and aunts would all come over and we would flat out have fun. His family was the absolute best! I could not have asked for anything more.

Now This Is Living

For the next couple of years, we were just doing us. We were doing things I had only dreamt about doing. We would go horseback riding along the beach, spend weekends away together in Carmel and Monterey, we would go on skiing trips, take family trips to Southern California to the amusement parks, I mean we were just having fun and enjoying life. One of the things I appreciated about him and our relationship was that he was very family oriented and this was a quality I so appreciated about him.

SIDE BAR: *See, I remembered as a child having the family environment during times when I was living with my grandmother. This all changed for us when she left her home and relocated to help a family member. I no longer had that family environment. It was an experience I had for a brief moment, but one I longed for long after. For years it left me in search of what I experienced during this time with my grandmother. After what I experienced living with my mother, this was an experience I seemed to be chasing even harder.*

With the life he and I had together, I just knew this had to be what would quench my thirst for family, for love and for happiness, at least that's what I believed. We went on living life and enjoying ourselves. Every holiday we would spend with his family at his grandparent's home and it would be filled with family, food, fun and laughter, and all so very nice. I could clearly see where he got his family values from. When my sister was in need of help and asked to come live with us, he asked no questions and this happened on more than one occasion.

When my grandmother came to live with us to have hip replacement surgery, again he asked no questions. In fact, he cared for her like she was his blood grandmother. The two of them had this lovely bond and she was absolutely crazy about him. When two of my little cousins, on two separate occasions needed to come and live with us, I did not get an "I don't want to be a father" statement, he actually wanted to be a father and welcomed them without any question. He treated them as if they were a part of his family and they were. This was the first time I saw what a healthy relationship was like and it was great to see. It was what a relationship and a marriage was supposed to be, right?

SIDE BAR: *Because something is pleasant in nature, does it make it the right thing? Because a situation has* *all the makings of a good decision, does it mean it was God's decision? Just a couple of thoughts.*

Because he was family oriented and it was a known fact he wanted to be a father, I was convinced he was going to be the father of my children when we were ready, and we were not ready. At twenty-two years old when I experienced the trauma of the tubal pregnancy, I wasn't really concerned with whether, or not I would be able to conceive again. The tubal pregnancy and the cir-cumstances surrounding that experience and becoming pregnant was the last thing on my mind. However, due to PID (Pelvic Inflammatory Disease), which is what you end up with after untreated STD's, my right tube was pretty scarred and part of it had to be removed. However, over the years following this experience doctors had given me a pretty positive outlook. I was told that my left tube was functioning normally and the remaining portion of my right tube could be easily repaired with a minor surgery, if needed. With this news, I was not really concerned about becoming a mother, we were simply having too much fun to focus on kids.

I Had Cause to Be Concerned

Around 1994 people within our circle of family and friends began sharing stories of baby bliss and with each new announcement of pregnancy, I was beginning to feel that desire to be a mom, too. I would start seeking out medical advice to make sure everything was okay. Over the next couple of years, I would frequently experience missed cycles, but I had not become pregnant. This occurred often enough that it began to be cause for concern for me. Especially since I had the ectopic pregnancy. From these experiences, I would begin a journey of various medical procedures and test to ensure there was not a problem that was preventing me from conceiving. With each new test, each new procedure and each new dose of medication the answer was always, we can't find any reason why you're not conceiving naturally. This was both good and bad news for me.

I became an undercover, possessed crazy lady trying to figure out why I could not have kids! Remember while living with my mother I learned the art of hiding what was really going on? Well, here's yet another area I put the little trick I learned to use. I never let my boyfriend, or anyone I was close to know I was truly possessed with trying to become pregnant. After more repeated tests, procedures, and medicine regimes of Clomid and other hormone pills, I started to feel ashamed and embarrassed that it was taking all of this to get pregnant. Like I was less than a woman. Worse, I felt like I was a piece of woman, because I could not do the one thing that seemingly came so easily and naturally to other women.

My body was not functioning as God designed it to and I didn't know why. I was now starting to believe the lies coming from the whisper of the enemy filling my mind. I was beginning to believe God was punishing me. After all, everything I read in the bible told of how children were a blessing from God. When your womb was blessed you were blessed, if your womb was cursed, you were cursed. It was right there in black and white and I was reading this with my own eyes. There was no debating with what I was reading, right? Why was God punishing me? What had I done that would warrant the severity of such a punishment? To these questions I had no answers. So I continued to search out the why?

SIDE BAR: *Reading the bible void of understanding from God can lead to a misunderstanding of his word. This was my experience in trying to interpret scripture on children being a blessing and not being able to have them as a sign of a curse. Reading the bible void of God's insight is dangerous. Always pray before you begin to read the word of God and ask God to open your eyes and to illuminate the scripture for you.*

While I was the crazy, possessed lady, my fiancé seemed to be fine and in no way concerned with whether or not I could get pregnant. His faith was intact and appeared to be very strong! He would tell me all the time "it will happen when it's supposed to." He was not the least bit concerned. In 1995, he planned this real elaborate event at the Embassy Suites in Milpitas where we had spent a couple of getaways and he knew I liked it a lot. He invited all of my family and the family I moved to Oakland with (my ex-boyfriend's family, because he knew his mother was like my mother), and all of my friends and he was going to proposed to me in front of everyone. That is until I blew his plans right out of the water with my "stinky" attitude. An attitude I had because I was "tired" of being and doing everything, with everyone all of the time. See, we were always with family and friends. I mean we did EVERYTHING together and at this point, I was yearning for some "us time." I learned of these beautiful and romantic plans after demanding we didn't do anything with anyone. Sadly, I didn't know the anything was everything he had planned, so at my harsh request, he called it off. Okay, so you know I tried to reignite the plans he was working on right, the plans for the surprise. It didn't work. He honored my request and he took me to Red Lobster for dinner, just him and I, and nervously proposed to me. It turned out to be just what I wanted.

After proposing to me, we would start making plans for the wedding and for purchasing our first home. He apparently had been looking around the neighborhood where we lived because he would drive me around to look at vacant properties so I could pick out the house I wanted. He was so considerate and kind. From all of this, I knew before asking me to marry him he had taken into consideration what it meant to have a wife, to be a provider, and to care for his family. This was eye opening for me. He had actually prepared to be married, even unto purchasing our first home. Take note, my beautiful sisters! I'll say it again: he prepared to receive a wife. He prepared to be a husband. A rare quality indeed! We continued to look for a home before deciding to take advantage of another opportunity for home ownership. Wow, could this really be real?

SIDE BAR: *I would like to reference a passage that is widely used, Proverbs 31:10, "Who can find a virtuous woman, for her price is far above rubies." I would like to focus on three words here, "Who can find?" When you* look at this phrase, what comes to mind? It's more than a simple question that's being asked. It's deeper than that, much deeper than that. Imagine your dad and he's going through the selection process, making his choice for a husband for you his daughter. In his eyes, "your price is far above rubies." Saul told David he needed 200 sheep skins for his daughter's hand in marriage. How much more are we worth to God?

He starts the question with the word "Who" in other words, who would be "the favored" of God, the blessed of God, the one chosen by God and hand-selected by God himself, predestined by God for you his precious daughter? Dare I add, someone was pre-selected for you before he placed you in your mother's womb? That's the "who" here! So it isn't just anyone God desires to release his precious daughters to! Then, the passage goes on to say "can find," this suggest this is going to take some effort, a little work is going to have to be done. This also suggest, this virtuous woman, is a "RARE FIND." Of her, there is no dime a dozen. Now when he say's "find," he's talking about the one he (God) wants to bless with his *prize possession; the apple of his eye, his princess, his precious daughter. Who is the one, the man, that can go and stand before God and say, "I am he, the one worthy of the rare find, the one who is honorable enough to be chosen by you God, the one who has found a good thing, the one who recognizes and understands her price is "FAR ABOVE THE PRICE OF RUBIES."*

I said all of that my beautiful sister's, to encourage each of us to know our WORTH and stop looking for the one who should be searching for the precious jewels we are. God has set him on a journey to find YOU! So when God asks "Who Can Find" he's asking if he can find the man worthy of you, his (God's) Virtuous woman. STOP SETTLING FOR LESS THAN WHAT GOD PREDESTINED FOR YOU! You're a King's Kid and that makes you a QUEEN!

NOTE: We need to study and understand who we are as Kingdom residents. God began to deal with me on this many years ago in 1992 and it was shortly after that I was introduced to Dr. Myles Munroe's work and ministry. He was truly a General when it came to educating us on

"Kingdom Living" and I learned a great deal more about living in the Kingdom from reading his books. You can only live as a King's kid, when you understand the King and his Kingdom! Get a Kingdom mindset!

No, Not Now

Everything was going great for us when shortly before our wedding, I began to experience the pull again. You know, the spiritual pull I talked about earlier? I thought, no, not now! Things are finally starting to work in my life. It's starting to mesh with what I know it's supposed to be, right? Why is this starting again? I thought go away and it wouldn't leave! With this pull ever so strong, I knew I could no longer resist it. What is going on with me? I am now starting to seriously wonder if I am really crazy? I would talk to my grandmother about what I was experiencing and she would tell me stories of those in our family who were called of God and I listened, but thought nothing of it. Meaning, I didn't think I was called of God and what did being called of God really mean and why would he call me? After all, did he not know who I was and where I came from and how messed up I was? He did know this, right?

My grandmother gave me some of her prayer books to read and they helped, but they did not stop the pull I was experiencing. This pull just became increasingly stronger, so much so that I would eventually have a conversation with my fiancé. I told him that I felt like I was being called by God and that I didn't know what this meant, or where this was going to lead me. When I spoke to him I wasn't saying I was being called of God like Moses or anybody, but rather I felt like I was being drawn into a deeper relationship with God. A relationship that I did not understand. I then asked if he felt like he could handle whatever this was?" To be honest, how could I ask him such a thing when I didn't even understand what it was I was asking him to handle? Nor, did I know if I could handle whatever it was God was apparently asking of me.

This was now starting to feel like a nag that wouldn't go away; an itch that I couldn't reach to satisfy. I mean come on, this has been happening since I was a child. Just when I feel like my life is starting to make sense in the natural, it's seemingly getting crazier from a spiritual stand point. As much as I tried to run, ignore and pretend the nudge wasn't there, I knew God was wooing me. I was attending church on a regular basis, like every time the doors opened and my fiancé seemed to be okay with it. It seemed whatever we both agreed we could handle, we appeared to be handling "it" just fine. My attending church hadn't change anything in our relationship and my fiancé wasn't threatened by my rebirth of Christianity. We moved forward with planning our wedding. We were married a year later, and seemingly having more fun together!

After we were married, he didn't want me to work (I know, who does this, right?); he wanted me to stay at home, but I had too much of an entrepreneurial spirit. With the support of my new husband and one of his family members, who was just wonderful, I took that leap and started an unofficial business. A year earlier, I had started designing t-shirts and mouse pads for clients, who were family and friends, and their referrals. I expanded on that idea in the graphics world. I also loved to write, so I started writing and creating my own greeting cards for family and friends for special occasions. I had started creating my own bookmarks from poems I had written and my best friend and I wrote our very first magazine together. I went on to further teach myself how to use the latest "Adobe" graphic design software, purchased a G4 Apple computer, and shortly after learning the software, I enrolled in graphic design school to ensure what I had taught myself was correct.

The Entrepreneurial Bug Had Taken a Hold of Me

After graduating from graphic design school, I started my own business called "Simply You, Designs from the Heart." I had no clue what I was doing, but I stepped out there and with my husband's support I secured a contract or two. I designed business cards, brochures and fliers for clients, family and friends. Before long, I started another business called "Graphix by Ceola" and began designing corporate identity packages for a couple of small businesses; designing logos, business cards, brochures and more. Discovering the creativity in me was fulfilling and rewarding. I enjoyed it. With both businesses, I was learning so much. I gained more wisdom and knowledge on how to start and operate your own business. Yep, the entrepreneurial bug had taken a hold of me and I was beginning to have a strong sense of who I was, what I wanted, and my destiny in life. There was no stopping me now!

SIDE BAR: *Little did I know this was all a part of the training ground with God for His purpose for my life. Believe me, it was not what I was thinking by a long shot! Isaiah 55:8 reads "For my thoughts are not your thoughts, neither are your ways my ways, saith the LORD. For as the heavens are higher than the earth, so are my ways higher than your ways, and my thoughts than your thoughts."*

It seemed with the entrepreneurial and creative spirit that was now active in me, I started feeling the pull even more, if that was possible. A few years later, my hus-band and I both would go through transitions on our jobs and as a result our marriage would start to suffer from what most marriages experience: financial strain. This was something unfamiliar to us. Unfortunately, it was also the beginning of a shift in our marriage, a shift that would bring more than we could have ever imag-ined, including my continued quest to become a mother.

They're More Frequent

In 1997 I started dreaming more frequently. I would hear peoples' names being called, those that I both knew and had never met. I saw places I had never been before, and events I knew were going to happen in the future. Even more prevalent were the dreams I was having about myself. Those dreams occurred in two part. One part of the dream would be of the old Ceola, that was usually separating and being left behind. The second part of the dream would be of the new Ceola being led by the light and moving forward. It was like I was being shown the past and the future, but with no details of the things that would happen in-between. Talk about requiring faith and trust.

How could I have faith and trust when I didn't even know what any of the dreams, or other spiritual experiences meant? For the next year or so, I would continue to attend church regularly and I was starting to have what I thought was a deeper understanding of spiritual things. With that came a desire for more knowledge of God. I wanted to learn and understand all I could about him. I was no longer satisfied with the "superficial" church experience. I wanted God on a more intimate level. I remember it like it was yesterday, I started asking God by praying this prayer, ***"Lord, there has got to be more to life than being born, growing up, graduating from school/college, getting married, having kids and working, only to retire and die! Please Lord, use me and grant me wisdom."*** I kid you not, that was my prayer. Where this came from, only God knows. I was no longer running from God, but I was running to him. I was now asking for more of him, rather than asking him to let me be and enjoy my new and happy life. I was seeking him and desiring to live a life of purpose, meaning, and significance. Now this was a shift! I was no longer afraid of the things that were happening to me, of the experiences I was having. No, I was now embracing them and wanting to understand them even more.

What Now, Lord

It was in the middle of 1998 when I was introduced to a woman who apparently had been on a spiritual journey with God, also. She became my introduction to spiritual mothers. In early 1999, after almost four years of attending church, I left the church and started attending prayer meetings at this lady's house. In the beginning of our acquaintance, she would invite me and the other ladies to prayer at her house on Saturday morning and after prayer, we would stay for lunch and fellowship. We would also attend bible study on Tuesday nights in her home. This started out as being a very nice time of intimate fellowship. It was also yet another total shift for me and for my life.

In mid-1999, I felt God was leading me and my husband to sell the condo and move. Although I truly believed and felt confident God was leading me, I still sought the counsel of this lady. After all, I had years of him wooing me and giving me dreams and visons of things happening just as he showed me. Why would I start to doubt now? I felt like God was directing me, but I was a little uncertain. After all, this was a big move for us and I did not want to make a mistake. Remember, we were already facing financial challenges, something that was new to us and I did not want to plummet us into anything deeper. After consulting with her, God gave me another dream of me painting our condo in preparation for the move. The colors were the strangest combinations of colors you could imagine.

Okay, are you ready for this? Here are the colors I was instructed to paint the condo: our master bedroom walls were lilac with yellow sponge painted on top (God help me). Our master bathroom was the same color.

The main bathroom was peach and white (it was pretty). The second bedroom was, get this, pastel green. But I built a shelf to divide the wall (top from bottom). The bottom was striped with pastel green, fuchsia and white. Each stripe was a specific size per color and the pattern continued around the entire wall of the bedroom. The kitchen cabinets were a natural maple wood with frosted glass. I removed the glass, sanded the cabinets down and painted them cream. The living room and dining room were powder blue and trimmed in cream. The fire place was trimmed in cream, with the inside painted powder blue.

When I finished, not only were people amazed that I painted the entire condo, but they were shocked at my color selection. Even I was baffled at what I had done. I felt stupid and embarrassed, but who could I tell God told me to do it? We listed the condo and began showing it. People came to view it, but there were no hits. Seriously, could you blame them? Who would want to buy a nice condo ruined with a horrible paint job? The painting was good; it was the colors I thought made it horrible. We received a request to show the condo one evening, and when the lady arrived, she walked in, looked around and said "this is exactly what God showed me." I was floored! Are you kidding me? She bought the condo, people. She bought the condo! The lesson here is to "obey God" regardless of how crazy it seems. Obey!

Back to Oakland

We sold the condo in late 1999 and I knew we were supposed to move to Oakland because God had given me another dream. This one showed me the exact street exit to take and he had given specific instructions of what my husband and I were to do. We were to go to this specific place to eat and when we left, we were to grab the newspaper from the box. It's pretty incredible now looking back. As we walked into the restaurant, my husband was reaching for the newspaper stand handle and I said, "No, God said to get the newspaper on the way out, after we eat." We did as he said, right down to which direction to exit the parking lot when we left.

Driving in the direction we were told to go, we arrived on a street not far from the restaurant where there was a "For Rent" sign in the window of the upper unit of a duplex. I'm not going to lie, I was amazed. I wrote the number down and called later that evening to inquire. The man who answered the phone (we'll call him Mr. Landlord) was an older gentleman and we talked for a few minutes when he asked me my name again. When I told him, he replied "that's my daughter's name." I thought surely, this man is old and clearly does not know what he is talking about. We discussed the home and ended the call. About 6:00 am the next morning, Mr. Landlord called us and said "If you want the place it's yours, just bring me $600.00." Not long after meeting with Mr. Landlord we agreed to take the place and moved to Oakland from Hayward. We also discovered that his daughter's name was indeed Ceola, the same as mine. Now I can see, Sarah, Michelle, or Mary, but Ceola? This was clearly God. How about that? In November of 1999 we would move to Oakland as God instructed.

SIDE BAR: *Most things God asks you to do will not make sense and quite often will make you look like a fool to people in general. But if you trust him, he will glorify himself. At this time, I could only share with a select few any of this, but look at God now. His is glorifying himself. In addition, he was teaching me how to hear his voice and follow his instructions, regardless of what I thought, what people thought or how it looked. He was more interested in my obedience! Just as he is in your obedience!*

PLEASE NOTE: For the sake of moments that are private with God, I will not reveal specific details of the dreams, but just enough for you to get the point.

I Cried and I Questioned

After such a wonderful experience with God painting the condo those crazy colors, him sending the woman to purchase it, providing the new place and favor with the new landlord, whose daughters name was the same as mine, I cried like a baby! That's right, I cried! After the excitement of hearing God clearly and moving with him, I woke up in the new place and realized where I was now living. My heart wasn't broken, my pride was! I was not living in our nice condo in the Hayward Hills. I was living in a duplex in Oakland that was old, out dated and severely run down! I was in shock! The duplex was a mess and I was an even bigger mess!

Before we moved all of our furniture into the duplex, my husband and his cousins were literally playing catch in the living room with a football. That's how big this place was. It was three bedrooms, two full baths, a family room, dining room and kitchen. Why did we take this place? Was it because God led us here? Was it because with my interior design mind, I thought this was the perfect project? I was now starting to question everything. Maybe I did not hear God correctly? Maybe the advice of this woman was wrong? Maybe the lady who bought our condo had her signals crossed too. Maybe this was a mistake on all of our parts. This could not be God! After all, he had blessed us with our first three-bedroom nice home and then a very nice condo in the Hayward Hills.

Everything was going great for us. But now, financial struggles and moving into this shabby duplex? What is happening here?

I was sure there was some miscommunication somewhere and this simply could not be God. This place had four different colored carpets that had not been replaced in like decades. The vinyl tile on the kitchen floor was very old and peeling up. The windows in the family room were so old, they were nailed shut! I remember the night I tried to open one of the windows before realizing they were nailed shut. This sent me into another crying tizzy. I cried and asked God what is happening to us? The second bathroom was pink; pastel pink to be exact! I thought when you give your life to God, things got better. It was not supposed to get worse, right? For us, it seemed as though all chaos was breaking out in our lives. Everything was starting to fall completely apart. The little beacon of light was Mr. Landlord worked with us on getting new carpet. Plus, he paid for paint so I could paint the walls and well, that made it a little better. However, we still could not get those darn windows in the family room to open that were nailed shut, nor could we change the pink bathroom. What could the lesson be in all of this?

The sale of the condo did bring a little financial relief. But over the next year my husband and I would continue to suffer financial hardships due in part to the transitioning of jobs and with reoccurring bills. Things were getting worse. My husband would get hired and let go from a couple of jobs. I was working a few temporary jobs before being hired permanently by one of the temporary assignments at a local hospital in 2000. Being hired by the hospital only intensified my desire to become a mother. Part of my employment requirements were to take annual continuing education (CE) courses and of course, my CE courses were on the female reproductive system. I immersed myself in this study. I wanted to know everything there was to know about the female anatomy and reproductive system. I wanted to be able to speak to my doctors with intelligence and I wanted to make sure they were doing everything possible to increase my chances of conceiving. I also made sure my insurance plans covered any potential infertility treatments, which back then were limited and expensive.

My Quest Continues

As I continued to seek medical counsel for why I was not conceiving, with each late monthly cycle I was being tormented by the harsh reality that I was never going to be able have children. I would never know what it was like to bear a child in my womb. I would never know what it was like to experience symptoms of pregnancy; cravings and yes, even the morning sickness. I wanted to experience morning sickness, that's how desperate I was to become pregnant! I wanted to know if my child would look like me, talk like me, think like me or act like me. I wanted to know what traits of mine they would have: eye color, hair color, etc. With each passing year, each new test, each new procedure and each new medication, I realized my chances of becoming a mother were growing dimmer and dimmer. My age was increasing and with it my dreams of motherhood were decreasing!

After years of going through missed cycles and negative pregnancy test, I became even more fixated on finding out why. I was checking out books in the library and conducting my own research. I made sure that each of my jobs offered the best PPO insurance so I could get the best medical coverage to ensure whatever test I needed would be paid for in full. I was totally obsessed with becoming pregnant. My doctors kept testing me and trying out new technology. My last doctor, exhausted at his attempts, referred me to an infertility specialist.

From this experience there were more test and more medications that were administered before my doctor suggested for a second time that my husband be tested. Well, I asked him and he refused. I was shocked and in disbelief, and I was hurt to say the least. I thought this is the one thing that can help me do what I want more than anything and he refuses. At the time, I was so fixated on becoming pregnant that I did not consider he may have been fearful of the results, too. It was all about me and how I felt. I believe this experience is one that caused me to harbor resentment in my heart towards my husband and unfairly and selfishly so.

I didn't want to admit I felt this way towards him. After all, this is the guy I was crazy about, the guy with whom I was having all this fun, the guy who I wanted to be my "baby's daddy" and now I am feeling resentment towards him. I simply could not believe it. After several months of asking him, he finally agreed to the test and all was well. This left me happy, but also sad as the results of the test offered no reason as to why "I" was not able to have children? There was simply no explanation. Every test came back yielding the same results and answers from the doctor, "you're fine. We're not sure why you're not able to conceive naturally." I stayed employed with the hospital for the next four years and I took total advantage of the benefits I had to continue to explore why I had not been able to conceive. As I continued my quest of becoming a mother, my marriage began falling to pieces. This was an unhealthy environment to bring a child into. Would that stop me from pursuing my quest? Keep reading, and let's find out.

Key Points:

- Season's do change. Don't get caught in the summer only having winter clothing. In other words, we can get so caught up in one season of our lives that we're not properly prepared for the next approaching season. Sometimes we can get so entangled in a situation such as a relationship, friendship, or job and just assume the good times, will always last, but they don't. Seasons change and if we are not paying attention to the "writing on the wall," we will find ourselves ill prepared for the next season in our lives and unable to shift smoothly.

- No Excuse. None of us have an excuse for ignoring the gentle nudging of God. We call these experiences dejavu, premonitions, daydreams, night dreams, etc. At some point in our lives, there is a gentle nudging, a moment when you know without a doubt God is nudging you.

- Can you recall moments in your life where God nudged you? If so and you have not yielded, now is the time you can stand up and say "present" God. As long as you have breath, it's not too late to answer the call, to yield to the purpose. Don't ignore the nudge of God, you never know when it will be his last time nudging you.

- Being led by God is rarely what most of us imagined the experience would be. I am sure of this fact. Personally, I imagined God would speak clearly to me and not give me steps that made no sense. Or, that I would have to follow in obedience, almost like a treasure hunt, with clues along the way. I thought whatever he told me to do would be effortless; no, that was not my experience. Everything God told me to do came with resistance and mocking. I thought professing that I assumed being a Christian and being led by God to do "Christian work" in the name of the Lord would give way to angels singing and favor granted. On the contrary, being led by God provided an opportunity to gain perspective and how to be steadfast. It increased my faith and trust in God, and I was able to see the effects of disobedience and so much more. Being led by God is not easy, but it is certainly priceless. I have No REGRETS

- Being led by God does not mean you will not encounter obstacles, or challenging times. Ask Jesus! What it does mean is this, like Joshua, we must go and do as God commands us, regardless of what it may look like. We must be strong and of good courage. We must not be afraid, neither shall we be dismayed by those who mock us. Or when being obedient makes absolutely no sense to the natural mind. God promised us in Joshua 1:9, He would be with us whithersoever thou goest. This means, wherever we go.

Questions:

1. Why does the truth seem to be so hard to accept, or is it?

2. It is possible for a woman to be blinded by the appearance of happiness because it masks the truth of her real pain? Have you ever had such an experience? If so, how did you handle it and what did you learn from it?

3. Do you recall moments where you were being nudged by the Holy Spirit and you ignore Him? If you think back, can you see where that act of obedience would have made a difference? Now I am not talking only deep here . . . what about turn left as opposed to turning right?

4. When we moved into the duplex and I really took a close look at what it looked like . . . the joy of the experience leading up to our moving was quickly erased. Have you ever had a moment, or moments where your faith wavered because what you imagined was very different from what you actually saw? How have you since grown from this moment and what have you learned from it?

5. Have you ever found yourself busy doing good works only to realized it was not God's work? How did you tell the difference?

6. Have you ever wanted something so badly that you found yourself possessed with the quest to get it? If so, how did you handle that situation? How can you help someone else who may be going through that same, or a similar experience?

Prayer:

Dear and wonderful Father, what an honor and privilege I have to come before you this day. There is joy in being able to enter into your presence with praise in my heart and on my lips. Your word declares in Psalms 100:4 *"Enter into his gates with thanksgiving, and into his courts with praise: be thankful unto him, and bless his name."* I bless you today for who you are, for all that you have so graciously done for me according to Psalms 100:3 *"Bless the Lord, O my soul, and forget not all his benefits."* I thank you today for your mercies that are new to me each day. I don't take for granted your tender care for me and I offer to you the gratitude of my heart this day. Father, I am so glad to have the many examples you have so freely given to me to help me navigate the varying seasons of life. You have shown me how to prepare for the change of seasons and I pray I would be more attentive to your teachings and I pray to behold the wisdom and knowledge you so freely share with me. Let me be as your word in Psalms 1:2–3 *"But his delight is in the law of the LORD; and in his law doth he meditate day and night. And he shall be like a tree planted by the rivers of water, that bringeth forth his fruit in his season; his leaf also shall not wither; and whatsoever he doeth shall prosper."* Grant me a deeper discernment Lord, to not miss pivotal changes in my life. Open my eyes that I may recognize when it's time to shift into a new season. Help me to be sensitive to the gentle nudging of your Holy Spirit and help me to be instinctively obedient to you. I desire to not grieve your Holy Spirit, so please Father, help me to yield to your precious Holy Spirit. In Jesus Name I pray!

Chapter 8

"To Have and to Hold or Not?"

"Wherefore they are no more twain, but one flesh.
What therefore God hath joined together, let not man
put asunder."
Matthew 19:6

The Next Eight Years

With the state of my marriage seriously on the rocks and with my silent suffering over my inability to become pregnant, I thrust myself into my graphics work and my gift basket business, which is picking up with requests from co-workers at the hospital. All of these things combined helped me to deal with everything going on. Plus, the relationship with the woman of the prayer group, whom I now called my "spiritual mother," was growing. It wouldn't be long before an unplanned "official" prayer group was formed and our house became "the" place where we continued to have prayer meetings every Saturday morning and Tuesday evenings for the next eight years. Yes, I said eight years! How, pray tell, did this happen? There were times when we would occasionally host the meetings at one of the other young ladies' homes, but the majority of the time we met at our house.

Is This for Real

For the first couple of years we met as a prayer group, it was really refreshing, fulfilling and rewarding. We were providing food bags to families in need and after a while we started supporting a well-known national organization for children. We were doing "good works" according to Matthew 7:21–23, *"Not everyone that saith unto me,*

Lord, Lord, shall enter into the kingdom of heaven; but he that doeth the will of my Father which is in heaven. Many will say to me in that day, Lord, Lord, have we not prophesied in thy name? and in thy name have cast out devils? and in thy name done many wonderful works? And then will I profess unto them, I never knew you: depart from me, ye that work iniquity."

We were growing spiritually, praying more, reading our bibles more and learning how to search the scriptures. We were taught how to prepare to present to the group when it was our day to host the prayer meeting. I mean how could this be wrong; we were being taught how to earnestly pray for others and how to fast properly. I mean come on, this was good, right? We were learning how to be true and supportive friends to one another, how to be Godly sisters and how to graciously and freely support others outside of our small circle. We appeared to be learning of God in a more intimate way; in a new and fresh way. Overall, we were learning how to reverence God. It was exciting to be learning about God from someone who seemed to have this amazing relationship with him. A relationship that appeared to be intimate and so personal. It was unlike any Christian relationship I had ever witnessed before. It was "deeper" than what I had seen or experienced in any of the churches I attended. It was something I personally had been desiring, so I was impressed, to say the least. I wanted to go deeper with God and so I took my love for learning and I willingly dove right in. Teach me everything. I wanted to learn all there was to know about God. I wanted everything he had to offer.

SIDE BAR: *But was any of this God? Why are some believers so easily wooed by people who look like God, act like God, talk like God and can even do wonders like God, but they are not of God? A tree is known by its fruit. Have you checked the fruit on the tree you may be sitting under lately? What, if any fruit is it bearing? Just because a tree produces fruit does not mean it's producing good fruit. Praise God, as Joseph told his brothers in Genesis 50:20 "But as for you, ye thought evil against me; but God meant it unto good, to bring to pass, as it is this day, to save* *much people alive." Is it possible that your struggle in life, your challenges, your trials, or tribulations were for a greater good? Something to ponder the next time you find yourself in a challenging situation.*

Sometimes God will allow experiences in our lives in order to glorify himself. In this prayer group and during this eight-year period of time, I learned a great deal about God, about how to dwell and tarry with him. If we don't learn to see our God in all things, we will miss the blessing in all things. Does not the bible tell us in Romans 8:28, *"And we know that all things work together for good to them that love God, to them who are the called according to his purpose?"* I am sure Job must have thought "what is happening to me and where is God" when his world got turned "topsy-turvy." We see from the beginning Job was recommended by God. I believe the question went something like this "Have you consider my servant Job?" How about you replace Job's name with yours the next time you find yourself in a storm, a trial, or a tribulation. Perhaps realizing God initiated your trial, may give you a different perspective and a better outcome.

Do we ever stop to think that some of the things we go through in life, such as attacks of the enemy are, our Father's recommendation? That God thought so much of us, that he actually suggested us for the trial? That he had so much faith in our faith in him, there was no doubt we would pass the test? Imagine that God, the great God and the creator of the universe actually sent a letter of recommendation to the enemy, and it began with two questions: 1) what are you doing? (Just in case we forgot who had ALL authority) and 2) have you "considered" my servant Job? Hmmm, I have you thinking don't I? Good. We so easily credit every challenging time to the enemy and it amazes me we do so without ever considering it just might be God at the helm. What if it's at God's recommendation? What confidence God, the great I AM must have in you. WOW, now there's a twist for real!

Remember earlier in the last chapter I said when you saw my husband you saw me? That was no longer the case. I had been introduced to observing the Sabbath Day by the woman in our prayer group. This meant I was no longer available from sundown on Friday to sundown on Saturday, including to my husband! I was an official Sabbath Day keeper, but I was not a Seven Day Adventist. Go figure. Yes, I was confused and in my confusion, I in no doubt caused a great deal of confusion to my husband! It became evident that this entire prayer group thing had finally begun to take a toll on my husband and on our marriage. My keeping the Sabbath Day meant I was no longer spending time with him and doing all the things we used to do together. I had adapted new practices and a new way of living. Some called our newfound way of life similar to that of an occult. Was it? I can see where that could have been easily assumed. There were things going on in the group that were probably not right. But anytime you yield authority of yourself, be it to another person, an addiction, or a belief system, you succumb to a dictatorship. Let's not confuse respecting authority with succumbing to a dictatorship. There is a difference. With all that my husband and I were experiencing in our marriage, we still tried to maintain our relationship, but is was far from what it used to be and was now presenting new relational challenges.

SIDE BAR: *It's amazing how we so easily become blind to situations; making excuses in some instances, justifying them in others. That's exactly what happened to us. The romance, the fun and the laughter was gone. You know it's sad, but it becomes really evident you're no longer loved when you find yourself recalling what is was like to be loved and facing the hard truth of who's to blame? There are always two sides to every story and I had to consider my role in the demise of my marriage. The truth is not always easy, but it is certainly liberating. Accepting truth is not a blame game, but rather an opportunity for growth and if those involved are willing, it provides a doorway to healing. I am happy to report, my ex-husband and I, are now really good friends.*

Strangely Odd

From a spiritual standpoint, this may sound strangely odd and I can only speak for myself, it appeared I was learning some things from being in this group. Being a part of this group as I said earlier, I found I was really studying my bible more and praying and fasting more. Recalling my statement in the previous chapter where I stated there had to be more to this life and that provoked me to ask that very question of God: Was there more to this life than the regular mundane cycle and then you die? I wanted to know if there was a purpose to life. Why did he create us? How is one fulfilled in him and in this life? I may not have liked a lot of the things that were going on in the prayer group. I did, however, gain a lot of wisdom and spiritual understanding from reading and studying the bible.

During the many Friday nights and Saturdays, I shut down and read my bible, a book or watched one of the many biblical movies I was introduced to. These movies were spiritually enlightening. I had never been in this place where I was studying this extensively. Nor had I been in a place where I was praying and fasting as much. During these times, my spiritual ears became more tuned to God. How could they not? You cannot earnestly seek God and not find him (Matthew 7:7–8). The circumstance in which you find yourself seeking God may not always be preferred, but the outcome is the same, you will find him. Ask Joseph. In a prison cell God was there. Ask Daniel. In a lion's den, God was there. Ask Shadrach, Meschach and Abednego. In a fiery furnace, God was there. Ask Paul and Silas, also in prison chains. God was there. Finally, ask Jesus, on the cross. God was there. Need I say more? The method in which God chooses to groom and mature us may not always be to our liking, but there will always be a benefit if we endure and persist.

Keeping the Sabbath Day taught me many things, some of which I appreciate to this day. I would have never learned how to shut down everything and spend amazing quality time with God. I also developed a routine for ensuring I was ready to enter the Sabbath on

Friday nights and this meant, dinner was already cooked. My house was cleaned on Thursday, only needing to be vacuumed and floors mopped, which I intentionally waited to do until Friday. After my floors were cleaned, I settled down, took a nice bath, lit a candle, listened to a nice worship song and entered into the Sabbath in prayer! The outside world was completely shut down! Wow, writing about this makes me miss this time as I no longer keep the Sabbath Day.

SIDE BAR: *Over the years I have come to learn it was not "keeping the Sabbath Day" I so enjoyed, it was what I was doing that I enjoyed and that was preparing to spend time with God; good, quality time with God.*

Imagine shutting the world down for one day. Not conducting any business, not doing any work, none whatsoever. Imagine having everything done, because all week you've prepared for the Sabbath Day. You're preparing to come spend uninterrupted time with God. Having worked toward this goal all week, when Friday arrives and you have nothing to do and nothing on your mind, this is an amazing experience. Trust me. When you come out on Saturday evening you are refreshed, revitalized, renewed, realigned and refocused for the coming week.

You just spent an amazing time with God in prayer and in worship with no outside influences whatsoever! Why would he not prepare you for the week to come? Would he want you to come back into the Sabbath the following week all beat up and stressed out? No, you're coming to spend time with him. There is nothing like the time you spend with God for an entire day with NO outside influences; no cells phones, no TV outside of a Christian or gospel movie, no music outside of Christian or gospel music, nothing of an outside influence. Even your conversations were different. The quality time I spent with God observing the Sabbath Day was one of the most incredible and precious experiences in my life! I had forgotten what this time was like. Writing about it is incredibly tempting to begin observing again.

Some may not agree with this statement, but for me, even though my marriage seemed to be falling apart in the last few years of my involvement in the prayer group, there was no denying the presence of God.

NOTE: I thought my marriage was falling apart because my husband chose not to serve God. I thought well, every man has free choice and he can choose to serve God or not, but I was not going to stop living for God! I figured I was praying and fasting for him, what else was I to do. See, the mindset I had was incorrect and my actions were not in alignment with the very bible I was reading and studying. In other words, I was not obeying God. There was a major conflict within me. I just did not have the wisdom, or the courage to follow the truth I knew. What I mean by all of this, is that my husband and my marriage should have been my first ministry, my priority, but it wasn't. If I were single, it would have been okay for the prayer group to be my priority. However, as a wife, your first ministry should always be your husband! Be careful who you are influenced by. If what you're being told does not line up with the word of God, it's not advice you should consider listening to. It doesn't matter who the advice is coming from. If the Spirit of God does not bear witness, do not take the advice! Today there are many people who know of God, and even have some form of godliness, but they are not of God. Please, don't make the mistake of following people! ONLY follow God. Seek God in everything concerning your life. If he is not present in it, you shouldn't be either!

There Is a Pain that Hurts Like No Other

It was in November 2002, shortly after recovering from back surgery when my husband and I would experience infidelity. For some months I was dreaming of people dying and warned about murders happening. These were not the only types of dreams I was having. I would also be awakened in the wee hours of the morning and given specific instructions to pray for someone. So for months I had this dream of a man being escorted in the nude out of a house through the front door by angels (my Lord, I have never shared this dream with anyone) and, for the life of me, I did not understand the total meaning. I mean the fact that the man was nude represented exposure . . . I knew that and the angels represented protection. I knew this as well. Overall, I knew God was providing protection from something, I just didn't know what.

My fax line in my home office was constantly ringing and this phone was rarely used. Being that I just had back surgery, I could not get back to the phone to answer it. This went on for at least a week when one day I was finally able to make it to the phone and to my surprise, it was a woman. She proceeded to tell me all about me. How I was a Christian and believed in God and so was she. She told me how she felt bad for me and she felt it only right that she called to be honest with me. Then she dropped the atomic bomb on me. She said I just wanted you to know that I am 3-months pregnant. My heart dropped and my pain was beyond indescribable. The life had literally left my body and I gasped for air. I could not believe what I had just heard. I was devastated! I had not relinquished my quest for becoming a mother. But now, another woman appeared to have what I so desperately wanted!

This incident happened just before the Thanksgiving holiday and represented the first time my husband and I separated. This separation lasted about eighteen months. While I don't condone infidelity, in all fairness, I must say this, when we open the door as I did with shutting my husband out and not spending time with him, I gave way to the enemy. Now wait just a minute, I know many of you have your mouths fixed to set me straight and there is no need for that. Let me say this, I DO NOT care what a person does, it does NOT warrant infidelity. My above statement is to make a spiritual point. We as women, Christian or not, should recognize that there are times when we can open the door, and give access to certain unfortunate circumstances to enter our lives. I am exhorting us as women to be as wise as a serpent, and harmless as a dove (Matthew 10:16).

SIDE BAR: *Just because an access point is given, does not mean it has to be taken! There is ALWAYS an option to say NO. To not enter in and to not engage. There is always an option to say NO and resist!*

Where Do We Go from Here

During this eighteen-month period my husband and I talked and spent time together. I mentioned earlier that I told him I understood how the prayer group interfered with our marriage and our household as a whole. While it did not justify his behavior, I understood how this could have happened, and I forgave him. I don't know, but after you experience something like this you start to think, was it my fault? Coupled with the fact I had just had back surgery and I just experienced infidelity, I felt it was necessary to stay in good physical shape. So I started exercising. I was doing everything from swimming two to three times a week, taking a Pilates class, body sculpting three times a week, walking around a nearby lake and running the stairs once a week.

It was not only for physical well-being. It was a way I could release tension and stress and also feel good about myself. Not to mention, I was probably running from the truth of what was going on in my life and marriage. You know how we as women do. Even those of us who are "strong." We bury ourselves in other stuff to avoid facing truth out of fear the truth might damage our image and our status. C'mon let's be truthful here. This is precisely what I was doing, but I told myself I was doing it for my overall-well-being. It sounded good to me, so much so that I had convinced myself of the lie. Have you ever been there? I wanted to bury myself in anything that would take me away from facing the truth of my current situation. I found was worked for me was over working, physical activity and shopping! Those were my vices!

At this time in my life I was offered to work with a client I conducted business with back in 1995 when I had my first business. I designed a brochure for his business model back then. He had finally gotten his business up and running and offered me the opportunity to partner with him. After careful consideration, I resigned my position at the hospital and went to work with him. It was not the thriving business one would imagine, but it had potential. When I went to visit the business, I thought am I really going to leave my job, which I was recently promoted and come to work here? The answer was yes, I would. Journeys with Jesus makes no sense to the natural man, but in the end, their yield is more profitable than one could imagine.

The business I had left my secure job at the hospital for was a start-up car detail center. I know funny, right? The owner had a big heart and he desired to start this business to help young men and women who had been recently released from prison find gainful employment. When I arrived on the scene, he had no computers in his trailer. Yes, it was not an office, but a trailer and not a nice trailer either! It was what looked like the smallest, run down trailer that was on its way out when someone said "hey, you want this" and he said yes, so they gave it to him. When I tell you he had nothing, he had nothing, but a great idea that could have turned into something magnificent.

After a couple of weeks of working at this detail center and seeking God in prayer and fasting, while with my prayer group. I made a few suggestions on how to grow the business as God led me.

We had the inside of the trailer painted and carpeted, bought a computer system, a mini refrigerator and got a water cooler for the workers and the customers. We purchased the necessary computer software, payroll software and made sure all of his legal (federal and state) paperwork was compliant. With these minor changes, business was starting to pick up and we were able to secure a couple more contracts with car dealers in the area, in addition to the contracts he already had. Business was so good that we were actually looking at another larger building to secure more work. While things were looking up for the detail center, I, on the other hand, had not been feeling well for the past few weeks. My energy level was down. I mean we were busy. We were picking up cars from dealerships, corporate offices and individual customers. Not to mention those customers who were Dropping their cars off. With all this activity I thought it was just the workload as to why I was so tired. But on the inside, I had this strong sense of knowing I was pregnant. It was not like those thousands of times before when I was pleading with God to let me be pregnant. No, I knew I was pregnant and I hadn't even taken a pregnancy test yet.

Shocked by the Results

When business was slow, I would get online and searched the many websites on symptoms of being pregnant. After years of trying, I knew all of the sites pretty much by heart and each one confirmed my suspicions. Armed with knowledge, the confirmation of the websites and my own physical body, I stopped on my way home and picked up a double pack pregnancy test, which had two separate pregnancy test. I took one test and after the first one came back positive; I took the second test. Shocked by the results, I returned to the store to purchase two more double packs to make sure it was accurate. I took five of the six tests and all were positive.

Shocked, scared, happy, excited and to some degree in disbelief, I sat down and cried, prayed and I questioned God. If this was really happening, I wanted to thank God for finally answering my prayers! I was finally pregnant y'all!

In pure excitement I called my sister-n-law at the time to ask if she could stop by on her way home and make sure I was reading the test correctly; she confirmed I was reading the test correctly and that all of the test I had taken were positive and I was indeed pregnant! After all this time and after being separated for almost two years, I was pregnant! This was in November of 2004. I was excited to be pregnant, but my husband didn't appear to be so excited when I shared what I thought was surely blissful news. He said he was, but I was not convinced. For the next few weeks I went on living the life of an expectant mother. Ooh, I was so happy! This time of the year was always my favorite time of the year and I loved to decorate so I was out shopping for all kinds of decorations and it was the best time ever! We planned Christmas at our house and had the tree decorated with ornaments reminiscent of a baby and we made the announcement. The family was elated at the news and it was a beautiful Christmas day until later that night when the light cramping and pulling I had been experiencing, which the doctor said was normal, started getting increasingly worse. On Christmas of all days, the time of the year that I love so much. Are you serious?

The next business day after Christmas I called the doctor and was told to stay off my feet, which I did. We would had tests run to make sure the pregnancy was what the doctor called "viable." That term did not sound good and along with the fact that we could not hear a heartbeat meant my worst fears were imminent. At my request to keep checking my HCG levels in hopes they would increase, the doctor finally said that is was not a viable pregnancy and suggested we schedule the D & C soon to avoid an infection. My world had just come to a crashing end! I felt like all hope was gone. I was getting older and my natural chances for conceiving was growing slimmer and slimmer. And in all honesty, I did not want to hear another person tell me the story of

Abraham and Sarah. This was my reality and I could not hold on to faith at this point. I was totally devastated. I cried when I left this appointment and I was angry and full of a million questions. I was doing everything right. I was praying. I was fasting. I was obeying God. I was helping people. I had not hurt anyone, yet. Why was this happening to me? I just didn't understand. If things could not get worse, before my scheduled D & C appointment, I began to experience pain unlike anything I had ever experienced in my abdomen area and below. Accompanied by heavy bleeding, I laid in my bed and experienced miscarrying at home. I wasn't even aware of such a thing, but that is exactly what happened to me! It was the most horrible experience ever!

I literary felt like life was leaving me and now I was once again questioning whether, or not I was being punished. Who goes through so much drama in one life time? One of my girlfriends was there with me for a little while, but at the worst point I was lying there alone. My husband had not moved back in yet so he was not there with me when it happened. I cried so hard and I felt like I was at my lowest point. I was ready to give up! It all had just become too much. I was lying there crying and thinking back over my life and once again I was left with a big fat question mark. The dreams that were coming all too frequent, the ups and the downs and all of life's twist and turns. None of it was making sense to me. No one's life can be this much drama! No one!

My husband accompanied me to the D & C appointment and, while I wanted and needed him there, I also didn't want him there. In addition to dealing with all the emotional disappointment, I was also feeling like as a woman and a wife, I had let him down. Even though I felt like he was not happy with me being pregnant, I knew he wanted us to have children. I knew what he was feeling was due to our marital situation and not the idea of us having children. I knew him well enough to know this. The entire D&C experience was like reliving the entire process of the miscarriage all over again. I tried not to cry during the process, but I kept on thinking why, why am I not allowed to have kids? Why would I get this close only to have the experience yanked from me? Why are you punishing me, God? Why? After the experience and all of the questions, I sucked it up, didn't let anyone know just how devastated I really was and I did what most of us women do. I kept it moving, without ever skipping a beat. Over the years I had bottled up so much pain, this was just another experience I needed to bottle up and keep it moving. Bottling up my feelings was something I learned as that thirteen-year-old child many years ago and by now, it was something I had mastered!

We're now into a new year and with the potential of business being even greater than the year before at the detail center, the owner sold the business and I resigned. With the miscarriage behind me, the detail center gone, I am now working on a temporary assignment and once again trying to move past everything that has happened. My husband is back home, but things are nowhere near right. At this point, we are more like roommates. I am feeling like the air was let out of me and just when I thought I was gaining some strength; I am deflated once again. What was God teaching me or was this God teaching me anything? What was I to learn from all of these experiences? What was there to be gained by all of this? Could it be to surrender? How about to increase my faith? Did my trust need to be anchored? Had I become too independent and not reliant upon God? Did God need to break my will and redirect me to accepting his will? What, why, how come? The answers would come later. Keep reading.

NOTE: It's interesting, as I am writing this I am reminded of a series of dreams I had between 2002 and 2005, which were of me fighting the devil. In the dream it was a spirit, but I knew he was the devil. Each time I won, but when I came out of the fight, I knew beyond the shadow of a doubt that I had been in a fight!

SIDE BAR: *Have you ever seen someone who had just come out of a fight? You know they won, but they looked disheveled. That is exactly how I looked each time and in each dream. In a couple of the dreams, I came out shouting the name of Jesus and huffing and puffing like I was tired! I believe these dreams were representative* *of all that I had experienced. It seemed like the devil was trying with everything he had to take me out. From a child looking back over my life, that it exactly what he had been attempting to do. Believe me, he was not finished. His attempts would continue. Let me summarize what has occurred since my transition to Oakland in 1984 up until the point of writing this book. Including topics, we'll cover in upcoming chapters:*

- *I moved away from home at the age of seventeen*
- *I experienced being in an unhealthy relationship*
- *Could have died from an ectopic pregnancy*
- *Took on the responsibility of raising my four-teen-year-old brother*
- *Went through a discovery phase trying to figure out who I was*
- *Considered suicide*
- *Ran from God*
- *Ran to God*
- *Got married*
- *Spent eight years in an occult like prayer group*

- *Unable to become pregnant*
- *Experienced a miscarriage when I did become pregnant for the second time*
- *Accepted I would never have children*
- *Experienced infidelity*
- *Committed adultery*
- *Went through a divorce*
- *The loss of material things*
- *The loss of my "so-called" status (surrendering my pride)*
- *Ensued the quest of God's will (seriously and not at my desire)*
- *Remarried and the rest will be revealed as you keep reading . . .*

The Torment, Fear and Desires of Suicide Resurfaced

By this time in my life, the pull I was experiencing and mentioned earlier had loosed me. I was no longer experiencing this. But why would I? There's only a need to pull something if there is resistance to it? My dream life was more active than it had ever been. I had just come through experiencing eight years of being involved in an occult like prayer group when I found myself committing adultery. Yes, adultery! Adultery is a very embarrassing and shameful act. It leaves you not knowing who you are. You question everything about yourself. Your integrity, do you have any? Your morals, do you have any? Your values, do you have any? Your self-worth and self-esteem are in question as is everything you ever thought you knew about yourself. When a person does something like this, it makes you question everything about yourself, that is if you're seriously seeking God. Yes, even in this state a person can be seeking God! I committed adultery and the torment, fear and the desires of suicide had resurfaced. I had sinned against God and I opened the door and had given the adversary access to my marriage and to me, again!

SIDE BAR: *Remember earlier when I said you can say NO? That you did not have to agree to engage, or say* *yes to ungodly behaviors and practices? That there was still an option and an opportunity to say NO . . . Well, I chose not to do neither of them. After being the recipient of infidelity, I said I would NEVER cause another sister (regardless of her nationality, religious beliefs, race, etc.) that kind of pain. No one should have to experience that kind of pain, no one! Guess what, I did it. I caused another woman that kind of pain!*

I found myself right back where the grace of God had rescued me from before, considering suicide. I was at a very low place in my life. I had known of two other ladies who were in similar situations and it was further torment for me to know what was right and yet lie and convince myself and others that what I was doing was right. How is a married man the one God has for you? Ladies, that IS NOT OF GOD and it WILL NEVER BE OF GOD. It is so easy to be hood winked and bamboozled by ignorance and the enemy. Let me also say this, we cannot blame the enemy for everything. God gave us wisdom, and he gave us the Holy Spirit, the Spirit of TRUTH. We know right from wrong. I knew right from wrong, so why did I continue in my mess? Why are so many other women who are in this sin, continuing in this mess, this lie, this bondage, this trap? If the grace of God does not snatch you out of this thing, it will snatch your very life. Why?

I remember the pain and the devastation I experienced when adultery happened to me. How hurt I was. How difficult it was to recover. How long it took to reestablished trust. I remember it all. What it does to you as a person, as a woman. Let alone what it does to you as a child of God. As a daughter of the Most-High God and an heir to the Kingdom? One of God's precious daughters? It makes you believe that you are not worthy, that God does not love you. That he will not forgive you. That you're doomed, dead on arrival and that you will never have an opportunity to come to God and ask for forgiveness and repent. Can I tell you God is a merciful and forgiving God? However, we must never take the grace and mercy of God for granted. We never know when enough is enough with God, so please don't play with your soul or with your life! The Father said to me a long time ago that "people will judge what they don't understand" and over the course of time I have come to personally recognize this statement as truth. People want mercy, but they are slow, if ever at all, to show or to give mercy to another!

It Hit Me Like a Ton of Bricks

I recall a time when a well-known Hollywood star was diagnosed with an incurable disease and I was sitting in front of the television when they were making their announcement. I can remember thinking and with an attitude I might add, why is it not until you experience something that a person wants to become a spokesperson and an advocate? I mean, I was pretty offended by their press conference. I thought about the people who have had this disease all along and now, since their diagnosis, it seems to be getting more attention than it was previously. Now the cause is getting much needed media and attention. I thought this was so selfish of them and so unfair to those who had been dealing with this disease for a much longer period of time. I can recall this today because that's how much their announcement affected me. However, I can truly say today, I am much more understanding, compassionate and merciful than I was back then. It's because of what I've been through that I have become an advocate for women. It's because of what my mother and I went through that as a child, my heart desired to start what I then called a homeless shelter for women and their children. You see, I did not understand that God has a permissible will in which he permits things for the greater good. I judged what I did not understand. Today, I understand that perhaps God allowed this in that person's life to bring forth what was needed for many more. Maybe he allowed Esther to be captured and taken to the king's harem to be prepared to be presented to the King to save her people. Let's no longer judge what we don't understand.

God is orchestrating a big world out there with a myriad of people. It's not that we are not important to him, because we are. But we must take responsibility for our own actions, and do so without being judgmental of others. We don't know what, or why a person does what they do, but God does. He tells us in his word to judge not, less we be judged. He tells us to love our neighbors as we love ourselves. He tells us to pray for those who despitefully use us. He tells us to turn the other cheek. He tells us that he would have mercy on whom he chooses to have mercy. Why would he tell us such things? We may never understand why people do what they do or make the decisions they make? Why they are the way they are? We are simply charged to love them. Does that mean we continue to be in the company of those who wrong us? No, absolutely not. However, we can still come before God on their behalf in prayer. The bible tells us to pray for one another (James 5:16).

All of us were not saints growing up, and well, by now you know my story and you know I was not. Sure, there will be those who cannot relate to my story, or the story of others and will not want to show mercy, have compassion, or yield forgiveness. But let me assure you, until you yourself have been in the need of mercy, compassion, and forgiveness, you will probably not be understanding. You can't give what you yourself have never received. I can give mercy, because I am a recipient of GREAT mercy. I can have compassion because I am a recipient of GREAT compassion. I can give forgiveness because I am a recipient of GREAT forgiveness. I can love because I myself am SO loved by God! Not sure of this fact, keep reading. God indeed is a very merciful, compassionate and forgiving God! My story reveals just how much of all these things he is and have been to me, and he is willing to be the same for you! Continue on.

Key Points:

- When we experience pain we tend to tense up. This is the body's way of protecting itself. This is exactly what we do when we experience emotional pain, we tense up, meaning we shut down, close the doors and refuse to let anyone in. We say, no one will have the opportunity to hurt us again. I praise God that this is not what I did when I experience the act of infidelity towards me. Because of

God, not me, I was able to see where I could have given access and invited the pain. We should pay attention to the invites we are extending and the access points we are giving the enemy.

- Sometimes when we don't understand or get the answer to our "why" questions we tend to draw our own conclusions. This is what I did when I could not become pregnant. I began to assume God was punishing me. I began to assume there had been a generational curse in my blood line. In my mind, clearly something was wrong. It never crossed my mind that perhaps this was not God's will for me. Yes, he said be fruitful and multiply, yes he said children are a blessing from God, but I don't recall where he said all women would have children. We just assume that in scripture.

- When we sit in the judgement seat you can hang it up! No one will ever receive mercy. Why is that? Why do we want mercy, but we're unwilling to give mercy? Why do we want God to love us past our sins, forgive us and help us, but we're not willing to do the same for others? Yes, I get it, adultery is bad and the sting of it is painful to say the least, but it should not prevent us from loving, praying and assisting as God leads, the person who may be in this situation. **WARNING**, infidelity/adultery has serious repercussions and can be deadly. Please, DO NOT enter these types of relationships!

- God always has a ram in the bush! During the time I was at one of my lowest points, it was a loving sister who nurtured me back to wholeness. She availed herself to God to pray for me as he instructed her. She informed me that God had laid it upon her heart to fast for me for forty-days. Are we availing ourselves like this to God on the behalf of others? What would have happened if she said " no Lord, I need to eat!" Where would I have been today? Would there be a book? Whose ram in the bush are you? Can you even identify who may have been your ram in the bush at some point in your life? Something to surely ponder on.

Resources:

1. National Association for Infertility—http://www.resolve.org/

2. Divorce Support Center—http://www.divorcesupportcenter.com/

3. Daily Strength is another website I found that offered information relative to miscarriage as well as information for other support groups concerning many other life issues, or challenges. To learn more, visit their website at http://www.dailystrength.org/

Questions:

1. Have you gone through a divorce? Have you recovered from it? How did you survive?

2. Have you experienced barrenness? Are you experiencing barrenness now? How are you handling it? Has it consumed your life?

3. Have you or do you know someone who has experienced infidelity or adultery?

4. Have you exhibited forgiveness? If not, why?

5. Have you noticed within yourself that you are a judgmental person?

6. If so, how do you proposed to change that or do you feel like you need to change it?

7. Do you desire to be more prayerful and more compassionate towards people?

Prayer:

Father God, the marriage covenant faces so many challenges and on every side, both from inside and from outside influences. This is why it is important for us to align ourselves with your words concerning the marriage covenant. Let us honor marriage and rest in the protection of your word in Matthew 19:6 *"Wherefore they are no more twain, but one flesh. What therefore God hath joined together, let not man put asunder."* I am praying not only for my marriage, but for all marriages, near and far Father God. Help me to see my marriage as you see it, Lord. Furthermore, help me to honor our covenant marriage that I entered into from the beginning as you instructed me to, per your word. Help me to continue to honor your way in marriage, and not the way that may seem right unto man. Father, help me and my husband to love each other as you have decreed in your word in 1 John 4:7 *"Beloved, let us love one another: for love is of God; and every one that loveth is born of God, and knoweth God."* Create in our marriage and our household Godly order as your word declares, Father. Help my husband to see the me as you see me, and to treat and love me as you have instructed him per your word. Help me to no longer follow tradition regarding certain scriptures, illuminate marital scriptures that I may see the truth of the scriptures and obey accordingly Lord, as written in 1 Peter 3: 7 *"Likewise, ye husbands, dwell with them according to knowledge, giving honour unto the wife, as unto the weaker vessel, and as being heirs together of the grace of life; that your prayers be not hindered."* And in Colossians 3:18 *"Wives, submit yourselves unto your own husbands, as it is fit in the Lord."* Help me to surrender to your will and your way. If my marriage has any brokenness, I pray you would heal the broken areas. If trust, hope and faith have been lost in my marriage, I ask you to restore them Lord and to help us to find a renewed hope in and through you. Restore lost love, renew and rekindle flames of romance that may have burned out due to the stress of life, financial pressures and any other form of distraction. Restore a love to my marriage that is grounded in and firmly upon your word. Breathe a fresh anointing on me and my husband and may that anointing fall to our children. Bring forth a newness in my marriage Father God, and let our marriage be one standing in righteousness and anchored in and on your word. Use my marriage as a beacons of light to all those who are considering marriage. We ask these things in Jesus' Holy Name, Amen!

Father, if I am barren in womb, help me to not only recite the story of the many women in the bible who found favor and hope in you, the God who opened their wombs, but let me find the strength and the faith to stand on the unfailing love and faithful promises of you, the same God who promised them and who will bring forth your promise in me. Let me learn from those before me and stand in agreement that the God who did it for them, can do it for me! Your word tells me that Hannah prayed for her son in 1 Samuel 1: 27–28 *"For this child I prayed; and the* Lord *hath given me my petition which I asked of him. Therefore, also I have lent him to the* Lord*; as long as he liveth he shall be lent to the* Lord*. And he worshipped the* Lord *there."* Let me not be double minded in my faith, but be anchored in my trust in you. Let me stake claim to your promises that are yes and amen! Let me seek you in spirit and in truth. Let me settle in my spirit that I am in agreement with you and your word. I believe you are a faithful Father. You are unfailing in your love and your promises again, are yes and amen. Remind me according to your word that *"Every good gift and every perfect gift is from above, and cometh down from the Father of lights, with whom is no variableness, neither shadow of turning."* (James 1:17). Comfort me as I patiently wait for you to act. If I have to go through the infertility process, give me strength and faith to withstand the process. I pray against failed attempts, miscarries and unhealthy multiple pregnancies. Help me to keep my head raised high through this journey and to continue in faith with you. Grant my husband the strength and faith to pray as Isaac did for his wife according to Genesis 25:21 *"And Isaac intreated the LORD for his wife, because she was barren: and the LORD was intreated of him, and Rebekah his wife conceived."* Continue to keep my husband and me in a spirit of faith! Strengthen our marriage that we fail not in this journey, but that we would become even stronger as a unified body. Dry our past tears and give us the joy of laughter! And Father, should it be your will for us to receive the gift of a child through adoption, open our hearts and our eyes to the honor you would bestow upon us to usher your child into their destiny. Help us to see our impact, our impartation, our love, and our faithfulness that would encompass the gift you would give us. Help us to see love is only deepened when we are willing to stretch far, and when we can open our hearts and not limit ourselves out of our own hurt and selfish desires. Help us to see love is needed by all and parenting is not limited to what is birthed naturally, but by what is given by God. Father, my prayer is not selfish and I pray for each parent and those desiring to be parents, that your will God, will be done. In Jesus' Holy and Precious Name, Amen!

Chapter 9

Redeemed: Grace + Mercy = Merciful Savior!

"Let the redeemed of the LORD say so, whom he hath
redeemed from the hand of the enemy."

Psalms 107:2

A Change is Coming

It is now early 2008 and my marriage appears to be
finally over. For two years now, I had been seriously
contemplating moving out and had been looking at
places to move. I openly shared this with my husband
and neither of us were happy about it. To be honest, I

spent a couple of years considering if I was making the right choice in leaving. I had never witnessed a healthy marriage before. I did not know where I should draw the line. I wasn't sure if I should "fight" for my marriage. I did not know how to look past the hurt and the pain and "hang in there." I did not know what I was supposed to do. I had no older woman who had been married and survived to tell me how she did it. **NOTE**: *Man, I wish the movie* ***"War Room"*** *was out back then.*

SIDE BAR: *We need more movies, more testimonies, more women coming to the forefront to help the young women.*

I needed someone who could show me how to do it. I thought I would be married to this man for life. I thought we would make it through the rough patches, no matter how difficult. As little girls and teenage girls we're sold this fairytale of marriage, motherhood and the ever after, but no one ever tells us the truth. The truth that there will be difficult times and times of devastating pain. Times of broken trust and times of tears. Because no one ever tells us this, we're never prepared for it. And when we encounter these marital challenges, we have no point of reference from which to draw. No solid guidance to make it through to the other side.

I never wanted to be divorced and when my husband and I married we both agreed that we would not get divorced. He would say things like "wife for life" and you know, I know he meant that. He was the kind of guy if he said it, he meant it. He was an all-around great guy. Unfortunately for us, neither one of us knew how to hold it together. Sadly, we separated as I moved out. This was one of the hardest decisions I ever had to make. I was ending a nineteen-year relationship. A relationship that started out great and that remained great for a long time. A relationship that ended up ship-wrecked and neither of us knew how to get it back on course. I am sure this was a very difficult time for the both of us. For me, there was just too much hurt, too much disappointment and too much pain to recover from. And I'm certain my husband felt the same, we had caused each other so much pain over time. As I shared earlier, people who have been hurt, often times turn around and hurt others. Unfortunately, in our hurting each other repeatedly, we dug a ditch that was too deep for us to come out.

SIDE BAR: *We as women who have the testimony of having a strong and healthy marriage and to those who have the testimony of not having a not so healthy marriage, must share with the women, young and mature alike. We must help them through marital challenges. It is crucial to help all who need the help, and all who are willing to accept the help. We do that by being transparent, by opening up and telling the truth. Having a heart of compassion, and not wanting to see another generation of "secret keepers," afraid to stand up and declare* **NO MORE** *and mean it. We need those who are willing to expose their lives so that others may have the opportunity to live in truth. Making a difference, requires taking a stand! Who's willing to stand in the gap? Who I ask?*

After the divorce, I threw myself into work to help me cope with what was yet another difficult time in my life.

In addition to working to help me cope, shopping was my other outlet for coping. With A Gift of Love, another business I started, I had bought a ton of gift basket products for the upcoming holiday's. I bought items for every key holiday. An old friend helped me at this time to categorize and inventory the gift basket product, which was a lot of work. We were trying to figure out how to market them when she suggested her cousin would be a good person to assist us in spreading the word. This is the cousin I met when I worked at the fast food chain some twenty-five plus years ago. The one where we both knew at the time there was something special between us when we met. We'll call him Miho. To move forward with our so-called marketing strategy, she reached out to him and asked if he would consider helping us to distribute my postcards and he agreed.

My friend made sure we had each other's contact information. It had been at least eight years since we saw each other. It wouldn't be long before we spoke. I shared information with him about the gift baskets and we agreed to meet briefly during a work break. At our brief ten-minute meeting we discussed the post cards and caught up a bit. We agreed to meet on our day off and catch up further. During this meeting we talked about the past, his kids, our families, my business, our marriages and the fact they were both ending. We reminisced about how over the years we would run into each other at various places and how we had helped each other out a few times over those twenty-five plus years.

None of these meetings were occasions where we would hang out, have coffee, or lunch. Nothing like that. We just thought it was odd how every now and again we would run into each other over the years. Knowing our history together, we both quickly stated we did not want to get into a relationship. He desired to stay single until his kids were grown and I desired not to get into a relationship because I needed time to figure things out. I was coming out of a nineteen-year relationship, an occult prayer group, recovering from infidelity, regrouping from committing adultery and trying to remain sane through it all. Entering into another relationship was not the solution. And we knew neither of us needed a new relationship. We both needed to heal and recover, or so we thought . . .

We Started Talking Frequently Over the Phone

Around May of 2008 he and I started talking frequently over the phone and spending time together. I had my friend back, the one who I could talk to about any and everything and we did. We shared everything. I told him all about what had been happening in my life and he shared the same with me. I was still living in the same house with my husband and it was November of 2008 when I officially relocated and separated from my husband. We had already been estranged and I did not believe our marriage would or could recover. At this time, my emotions were all over the place. I was ending my long time marriage, ending my long time involvement with this occult prayer group and recently reacquainted with a longtime friend. What in the world is going on? It was like I had been on this crazy roller coaster ride for far too long. My life was just on this crazy world wind and it seemed to be reshuffling and I had no clue where it was going to end up, or what state I would be in through the process and at the end of it all.

Seriously, I thought what is wrong with me? In early 2009 Miho moved in with me. Although we were both separated from our spouses, we were not divorced, hence another act of adultery. Again! Legally separated or not, this was not a relationship that was in Godly order and according to the courts and the law of the land, we were still married! I don't care how familiar the spirit is, the person is or how right it seems, infidelity is still infidelity and it is still WRONG and there WILL BE REPERCUSSIONS! Don't be fooled women, don't be fooled. If it appears all is well, don't be fooled. God being quiet does not mean his approval of any wrong doing! I don't care how right if feels, it's WRONG! If you are reading this book and you or someone you know is in a relationship that is not right biblically, get out! I am not talking about what your friends, pastor or your peers may say, or anyone else for that matter, including your sisterhood. I am talking about what the Word of God clearly says. It's there, read it with an open heart, an open mind and an open spirit. Seek the truth, it's there. You will find it in Hebrews 13:4 *"Marriage [is] honourable in all, and the bed undefiled: but whoremongers and adulterers God will judge."* It also states in Exodus 20:14 *"Thou shalt not commit adultery."* GET OUT OF THAT RELATIONSHIP!

SIDE BAR: *I am being honest with you as I share things I experienced because I don't want to see another woman go through unnecessary pain, or make the same stupid decisions and ignorant choices I made. Doing so will ONLY cause you heartache and pain, trust me! FLEE from sin! The results are more painful than you can imagine. The torment your spirit goes through is nothing like you can imagine. When I spoke earlier in chapter eight about opening doors during the process of adultery, this was a part of that experience I was referring to. DO NOT COMMIT adultery my dear sisters! PLEASE DON'T!*

Two Broken People Cannot Make a Healthy Whole

Having committed adultery again and with the one I called my friend, it would not be long before we would begin to experience our own troubles in our so-called paradise. You can't make two wrongs right—I don't care how you try it! Two wrongs will never make a right! Although our troubles were short-lived, they were very difficult, very painful and had laid the foundation for some very challenging times. Although we were able to recover and get through them, it would not be an easy journey and with it came many hurdles and hard times as a result of the decision we both made. Sin is easy to walk into, but hard to come out of and the residual effects can take even longer to come through! The entire process of recovery in any relationship takes a while. I don't care what the cause of it is, it still takes a while. It's a lot of hard work, and may require the help of out-side counsel. If your marriage needs counsel, please seek God in prayer and get it. Don't allow pride to rob you of the help you need. Miho and I were not married at the time, so this was not an option for us.

It was during this time that I learned two broken people cannot make a "healthy" whole. A lot of times people who are broken think they can heal themselves by getting into a relationship with another person. Unfortunately, they look to that person to make them whole. That can't and will not happen! A broken person cannot heal or make another person whole! Only God can make us whole. I believe this is one of the reasons why we have so many broken relationships and friendships. People never allow themselves the adequate time to properly heal. This is another area where I believe Miho and I made a mistake. We both went from one relationship, right into our relationship, trying to find wholeness and happiness. What we needed was to allow time for our own healing to take place, to get our marital situations resolved and possibly take some more time to allow those wounds to properly heal. Then, we could revisit the possibility of entering into a relationship with each other. God is the glue in all Godly relationships. He is the foundation and you can't truly have a well-rounded, happy and whole Godly relationship without God being the foundation on which it is built! Sorry, but that's the truth! Wholeness comes from God and God alone. When you're whole, you will experience happiness. Neither of these will ever be found in another person. Happiness can only be shared with another person, but it's birthed from within you, from your relationship with God, the Father. They both originate from the inside out, not the outside in.

There Are Consequences for Your Actions

I was praying, attending church and believing God, but I was nowhere near being obedient! I knew right from wrong and for a period of time prior to my left-winged actions, I had been experiencing many wonderful things with God. I mean I knew God and I had an intimate relationship with him, so why did I go on a quest of disobedience? Abraham had an intimate relationship with God when he told Sarah to lie to Pharaoh and say she was his sister. King David had an intimate relationship with God when he had an adulterous relationship with Bathsheba, got her pregnant and killed her husband Uriah to cover it all up! In both of these instances, there were consequences for their disobedience. In the end, and in both instances, God's will, will still be done, but why do we have to take the hard road when we can take the easy road? The one of total obedience? There are consequences for your actions as I said earlier and there would be many for us as we continued down this path in this ungodly relationship. And, so it began. I was laid off from my job; twice. You name it, we were experiencing it. You can try and pretend that you don't know what's happening and why, but if you're living in truth, you know why. We ALL have the spirit of truth on the inside of us and we all know when God is whooping us, trust me!

Finally, I just got to the point where I said, "You know what? I surrender. This has all got to stop!" I couldn't do it any longer. You can continue to make excuses and blame all that you are going through on the enemy, but that's a BIG FAT LIE. You can continue to go to church and think that God is blessing your mess, but he's not! For a while, things will look like they're going well and it will look like you're being blessed, but again I tell you, God's silence does not suggest his approval. Please take heed to these words. All that we were going through was at our own hands. We did this to ourselves. We invited all of this in by way of our sin before God. There are no if's, and or but's about it! The woe is me syndrome was not working here any longer. At some point you have to put your big girl panties on, yes, I sad "put your BIG GIRL panties on" and start dealing with the truth of the matter. Yes, we all go through and some worse than others, but these occurrences do not give us the right to act out and dishonor God. I am merciful indeed, but I am also a person of truth and I had not been living in truth! Again, I can tell you all that I was going through, had gone through, but enough already, Ceola. I had to get to the truth and the truth was I WAS WRONG—that's IT, that's ALL! I was doing what I wanted to do and justifying it by all that I had been through. The lies had to stop, the pity party had to stop! The poor little ole me, had to stop! The I am broken and weak crap, had to stop! If I did not truly surrender to God, He was going to put a STOP to it for me and that could have meant my life, literally! Continue to play with God if you want to! I chose not to. Praise Him!

If am a believer in God and his word tells me to let the weak say they are strong. It says I will live and not die! That greater is he that is in me, than he that is in the world. That I AM a word spoken out of the mouth of God and I WILL NOT return unto him void. It tells me that God is not a man that he should lie and that if he said it, shall he not perform it? It goes on to tell me that no weapon formed against me shall prosper, and that every tongue that rises against me, he shall condemn. I was at a point in my life where I was either going to believe the Word of God, or give up and DIE. I had to choose faith over fear, and rise up and be the fighter God created me to be. I had to make a choice and I chose life! This was a defining moment in my life. A moment of truth that would set the course for deliverance and healing.

I had not come through all that I had come through because I was weak. It was because the greater one was inside of me. It was because there was a purpose for which I was born, a reason for my living and breathing. I was no longer going to sit idly on the side lines and let the life God had graciously given to me, to be lived in vain! This all had to begin with me coming to and admitting the truth. No longer cowering behind guilt, shame, embarrassment, self-pity, and more. But rather being bold and confident in who my God was and is. This had to begin as I said with me first acknowledging what I had done in truth before II could get to my much needed deliverance! I had to be bold enough to live my true authentic self and that can only be accomplish by first accepting accountability and responsibility for my actions. Then I could begin the journey of living in truth! Once I did this and over the course of time, I began to share my experiences with all the women I spoke to on a regular basis, as I frequently had the opportunity to do. Initially, not knowing my life experiences, the women came to me to for advice, or spiritual wisdom (get that,

God has a sense of humor. He had them coming to me for advice. WOW). I thought I was sharing my experiences because I felt like I needed to let them know who I was. Isn't that sad? I began to believe my past actions now defined who I was. I did not believe 2 Corinthians 5:17, *"Therefore if any man be in Christ, he is a new creature: old things are passed away; behold, all things are become new."* The Word of God also tells us in Romans 5:8 *"But God commendeth his love toward us, in that, while we were yet sinners, Christ died for us."* How could I not believe his word?

The Lack of Mercy Revealed in the Most Unsuspecting Manner

In transparently sharing my story, specifically, the adultery. I begin to understand on a much deeper level how this particular act revealed the lack of mercy in people. Warranted, adultery is wrong as two left shoes and it causes so much pain. My God I know, because I've been on both sides. Let me just share this with you my beloved readers, most people would more quickly show mercy to the murderer of a child, than they would to a woman who committed adultery. A woman who has committed adultery is looked down upon, frowned upon, spat upon and left all alone! But, do you recall that Jesus did not leave her alone? Whether it was adultery or another form of sin.

When she, the adulterous woman was caught in the act of adultery, Jesus did not judge her. Instead, according to John 8:10 *"When Jesus had lifted up himself, and saw none but the woman, he said unto her, Woman, where are those thine accusers? hath no man condemned thee?"* In Luke 7:37–38 *"And, behold, a woman in the city, which was a sinner, when she knew that Jesus sat at meat in the Pharisee's house, brought an alabaster box of ointment, and stood at his feet behind him weeping, and began to wash his feet with tears, and did wipe them with the hairs of her head, and kissed his feet, and anointed them with the ointment."* Why is it in each scenario we see or read about it in the bible, Jesus showed such mercy? Was it the condition of their hearts?

Is it possible that some and not all women who are in adulterous relationships do not want to be in them? Is it possible for a woman who is in this situation to earnestly cry out and want to get out? Now, be careful how you answer these questions. Remember, people judge what they don't understand. If you have never been in such a situation, it may be difficult for you to demonstrate compassion. Maybe you just don't get it. Maybe you are that woman who would never do such a thing and who can't even begin to imagine or understand how any woman could do such a thing. Yeah, so was I. The answer to the questions above is the why behind the what! Jesus saw her why. He saw why she did what she did.

I am AMAZED at how critical and judgmental we as a people are. ESPECIALLY some of us so-called Christians. We are so much quicker to condemn people to hell, than we are to show them mercy. Now just because I committed adultery, does not mean I condone the behavior, let me be extremely clear about this, **I DO NOT** condone the act of adultery. It is wrong as wrong can get and **I STRONGLY** encourage anyone who is in an adulterous relationship to immediately get out. If you need help to get out, seek it! It is a sin and there will be repercussions for your actions, trust me. I know first-hand what this does to the one engaged in it. The mercy of God, does not mean there will not be repercussions. Let's not mis-understand this fact!

Like any other sin, committing adultery leaves you messed up in every possible way. In regards to adul-tery, or any other ungodly relationship that goes against God's word, we should obey the word of God and stay away from any and all "ungodly" relationships. I don't make excuses for what I did; it was wrong and I cannot express that enough! I do not agree with the statement "I found myself here." The truth is, like me, most walked into those relationship knowing right from wrong. We agreed with the terms and the conditions and we allowed it. That's the bottom line! The word tells us in John 8:32 *"And ye shall know the truth, and the truth shall make you free."*

SIDE BAR: *Not all like me will be directed to share as I have shared so openly. And trust me, as I said in the first chapter, this was not easy for me to do. Being open and transparent is a very scary thing. It leaves you vulnerable to all kinds of judgement and condemnation. It may make you feel lonely as people do not want to be associated with someone who is considered "tarnished." Or, someone who may have damage their reputation or hindered their opportunity to gain status or recognition. Taking a stand with God and trusting God to this degree is hard. But when your heart burns to truly help others avoid pain you've experienced, while the apprehension is still present, the compassion is even stronger. To whatever degree God directs you, don't deny someone the help God has provided in you. Whatever you've gone through is not just for your benefit only. Remember, the word says in Romans 8:28, "ALL things work together for good to them that love God, to them who are the called according to his purpose." And the "good" purposed for you can bless someone else too.*

As I said earlier, before we can come to a place of repentance, we must to come to a place of truth, and to get there we have to be willing to acknowledge the wrong we've done. No matter the circumstance, we still have choices to make. Let's own up to the wrong choices we've made, and go forward choosing what's right in truth. We can't get to real living until we get to the real truth! We can't fool God and we can't continue to be foolish enough to think we can play on the mercy strings of God Almighty. He is God! Remember that!

Let's at least have enough reverence for God to be truthful. No more lies, no more playing games, no more! I was in a really bad place for a time. I was emotionally tapped out, spiritually depleted, stressed and depressed, but I knew right from wrong. I chose to do wrong, then begged God to get me out of the mess I willingly walked into. Some of us women are bound by lies, bound by strongholds and more, but only facing the truth of what we've done to open the doors to sin will lead us to repentance, and ultimately deliverance. That, my dear sisters and friends, is the absolute truth!

God Will NEVER Give You Another Woman's Husband

Please, do not get involved in any ungodly relationships! When you do, do you really understand what you're doing? Do you understand that adultery is not divinely orchestrated by God? God will NEVER give you another woman's husband, regardless of what lies he may tell you, or the lies you may tell yourself. An adulterous relationship with a married man will NEVER come to pass. NEVER! Even if you believe it should have been the two of you that were married, and that he married the wrong person. God will not condone your relationship with another woman's husband! And NO, this does not mean the marriage should be tampered with by you, to help God release him from what you deem as a bad marriage. No woman should EVER interfere with another woman's marriage. Doing so will destroy families and hurt everyone involved! This should NEVER happen. ADULTERY IS NOT OF GOD and the word of God tells us that God will judge the adulterer. Again, I warn you to be careful, God will not be mocked!

When I committed adultery, I was sorely embarrassed at what I was doing and ashamed at who I had
become. But I did not stop doing what I was doing. After
it ended, I was scared to go out in public because I sus-
pected everyone knew what I had done. They knew my
deepest and most embarrassing secrets, and they were
all looking at and judging me. I was afraid to establish
close relationship with anyone. I was so paranoid with
fear that when I was around other women, I assumed
they were all grabbing their husbands out of fear being
in the same room with me. The thought of this hurt me
to my core, because I knew the act of adultery was the
furthest thing from my mind. I knew this behavior was
my past! Unfortunately, the people who knew what I
had done, chose to judge me wrongly! Sadly, I struggled
badly with the condemnation of this sin. The heaviness
of all of this caused me to want to commit suicide again.
For years I functioned in total fear of what would be
discovered about me by others. It is the most horrible
place to be and believe me, you do not want to be there
so please, do not do this!

We all know what women who commit adultery are called, how they are viewed, and the condemnation and the reputation that follows them. Look at those in the bible who were caught in the act and how they were treated. It's no wonder why those found in this situation often times consider suicide, or become bitter or hateful. I know, we could easily say, well they did this to themselves. To a certain degree, this is true. But, it does not mean they are not in need of mercy. They need help and the support to get through these situations. If they are repentant, and they are seeking forgiveness and the opportunity to turn their lives around, perhaps forgiveness and mercy should be extended to them.

Everyone makes mistakes due to bad decisions, and regrettable choices. I did. How is it that we so easily forget that we are ALL Sinners saved by grace? Why is it that the woman we walk past, who doesn't speak to us, is so easily assumed to be hateful, rude, or worse? Did we every consider it may be because of what she may have experienced? Remember, I said there is always a cause and an effect. Who knows? Maybe her pain is deeply rooted by a childhood experience. Maybe her hus-band cheated on her. Maybe she is the one who cheated and is considering suicide as a result of feelings of guilt and shame. Have you considered inquiring of God when you come across a sister who appears to be rude. Perhaps, she is hurting and displays her pain in a way that may not be so identifiable to you? Inquire of God and not people, and don't judge them. Inquiring of God is also called prayer. We need to pray for one another more and do less talking and gossiping about each other. It's prayer that will change things—not our gossip or judgement. People are in need of God's power to change them instead of the tongues' power to tear them down. Please pray!

SIDE BAR: *I was one of those women who walked around on autopilot with a fake smile on my face at work. Trying to do my job to the best of my ability and trust me, my work was suffering because of what I was dealing with. I was dressed to the nines, smelling good, looking good and doing everything as right as I could, considering all* *things. But can I tell you I was jacked up! Can I tell you that on most days I cried on my drive in and on my drive home? Can I tell you the level of guilt, shame, frustration and embarrassment I was going through on a daily basis was unbearable? And through my façade, all I wanted to do was end my life! This is not even my nature, but guilt and condemnation ae powerful tools of the enemy!*

I am sharing with you a story I read from a book I am sharing with you my intimate details of own life experiences. The issues we women encounter in life are real. The woman sitting in the cube next to you, she could be hurting in ways you can't even imagine. The woman who pulled up to you, smiled and spoke as you both dropped your children off at school, or the daycare, she may be depressed and masking her pain through drinking heavily. The woman standing in line in front, or behind you at the grocery store, she may be in an adulterous relationship and too embarrassed to tell anyone or seek help. The friend you talk to, every day, your so-called best friend and sister-girl, she may be hiding some things she is too afraid to tell you, her prayer partner. Get that! Pain and hurt are being disguised by people in new ways every day. Without deep prayer and unconditional love, pain will continue to remain hidden and women will continue to suffer in silence. We have to wake up and pay attention. We really do!

On the Verge of Overcoming

God revealed the power of overcoming to me in Revelations 12:11. He further expressed it to me when he told me that I did not believe in the cross. I was shocked by this revelation. I thought to myself, "but, of course I do"! I soon realized that not only did I not believe, but I lacked knowledge of what Jesus' death on the cross truly represented. With this knowledge, I would have not only known, but accepted that all of my sins, past, present and future, were already forgiven. That *"There is therefore now no condemnation to them which are in Christ Jesus, who walk not after the flesh, but after the Spirit"* (Roman 8:8). To not believe in the cross meant I didn't believe in Jesus Christ! This rocked my world.

This meant my going to church regularly and the eight-years of keeping the Sabbath and all my praying and fasting was without true knowledge of who my Savior really was. I needed to accept the truth being revealed, because my perception could land me somewhere even more dangerous. I must be careful not to let pride cause me to reject the truth. I must welcome it and seek what's needed in it and through it. Can I tell you, you will have to come to many truths in your life time and this was a hard truth for me to accept? Pride could have easily robbed me of my oncoming deliverance! Pay attention and willingly accept whatever truth God is revealing to you. Your blessing may just be wrapped up in your willingness to accept the truth! Eyes open, heart receptive and spirit willing, this should be your posture concerning God!

I had to consider what God was revealing to me. Upon seeing what I believe God desired me to see, I started asking God questions: How many of believers feel this way about the cross?? How many are going through the religious motions, the religious theatrics, the church protocol, the traditions and never really experience the intimacy Christ offers us in a relationship with God the Father? One would have to be humble before God to hear and accept such truth. We must be careful to never let our positions and our so-called status get in the way of us hearing and obeying God. Doing so, can result in us believing we can accomplish things without God. This thinking can cause us to move further and further away from God. Never having a real relationship with God your creator. God was right! What this all boiled down to was I did not believe I was worth being saved. That God would forgive me, or have mercy on me. I really didn't believe in the cross! This was an astounding revelation to me, and a revelation I so desperately needed. I did not believe in who Jesus was to me, what Jesus had done for me. This was basically what God was saying to me when he said I did not believe in the cross. This was a hard pill to swallow, but that's only because I hadn't swallowed my pride first! Swallowing pride makes it's easier to swallow the truth!

When I finally understood this revelation, I mean really got it, my entire life changed. And, for the first time I was able to freely accept the love God had for me, the same love that he has for you! It was not a love that required me to work for it. It was a love freely given for my acceptance. It was because he first loved me and that divine love was shown on the cross. You can't receive the love of God without first truly believing in the cross. With this revelation, I began sharing my testimony freely. All of it, including the adultery that for years had me bound with fear, guilt and shame! The enemy tried to use the shame to take my life, but praise God he did not succeed! God knew what he had purposed for my life. Now, I am a testament of his goodness and his faithfulness, his grace, his mercy and his unfailing love. I will forever share it through *my testimony. It's a testimony of Jesus and who he is! "For unto us a child is born, unto us a son is given: and the government shall be upon his shoulder: and his name shall be called Wonderful, Counsellor, The mighty God, The everlasting Father, The Prince of Peace"* **(Isaiah 9:6)**. I praise God for each experience, good, bad, or indifferent. It is because of each one that I am who I am today and I am finally happy being me! Yes, my dear readers, I know beyond the shadow of a doubt it was by the blood of Jesus that I made it through and this is my story of overcoming! To God be the Glory! Keep reading.

Key Points:

- Change in any form is never easy. When I realized my marriage was over, this was a hard transition to make and a very uncomfortable one. Always seek God before you make a life altering decision or choice. When you seek God, you have the comfort of knowing God is leading you and wherever he takes you, you know it will be all right.

- Sin can enter into your life very subtly and through familiar spirits. My Miho was a familiar spirit and even though I knew wrong from right, I willingly entered into an ungodly relationship. Get this, because I knew God probably more than he did at the time, does that or did that make me responsible for leading him into sin? Carefully consider your actions. Sin is serious, it's real and it can be deadly. Think twice!

- Mercy, greatly needed and sparingly given. This was hard for me to witness and experience. What's interesting is it was not hard for me to withhold mercy when I thought I was all that! Life has an interesting way of turning the tables. Be careful how you treat people. One day you may find yourself in need of the very thing you denied another. Careful, I say!

- God will NEVER, EVER go against his own word! He will not give you another woman's husband! Please, don't be ignorant of this fact. Resist the devil and he will FLEE.

- I learned as I said that two people who are broken can and will never be able to come together in wholeness until they themselves are made whole. God said and the two shall become one. He did not say the two halves shall become one. Never enter into a relationship with someone whose spirit is broken. You should never enter into any relationship unless God is leading you and he will never lead you into anything that is going to hurt you! Be wise!

- Consequences are the results of one's actions. When Miho and I willingly cohabitated while married, there were a plethora of consequences. Take note of what you will absolutely experience when you willingly walk in disobedience to God. Believe what you may, call it what you may, the truth is the light. Remain in darkness if you desire. Eventually, you will come to the truth. The question is how will you arrive there? In what condition will you be?

Resources:

Please refer to the back of this book for available resources and links to helpful websites.

Questions:

1. Have you found it difficult to change or transition your life? If so, how have you bounced back or have you?

2. Are you considering entering into an extramarital affair? Why? What is driving you to consider this as an option to happiness?

3. Have you experienced depression from choices you made and are those choices still haunting you? If so, have you sought help?

4. Has God revealed to you something you've had a hard time accepting? Has pride kept you from receiving the help, the truth, or the answer you need?

5. Do you have someone in whom you can confide in? Someone you can share the truth with, without being judged?

6. Do you have a regular prayer partner? Someone you know truly loves God and who will sincerely and earnestly pray with you?

Prayer:

Merciful and gracious Father, I come to you now in the name of our Lord and Savior, Jesus Christ and I come asking that you would provide me with the wisdom and knowledge to transition out from where I currently find myself. I pray that you grant me peace in my inner man as I transition with you. I ask you to show me your will for my life and grant me what is needed to land on solid ground. I also come praying that you forgive me and deliver me from my sin. I pray for my own soul today, Lord. I pray for my own mind today Lord. I pray for the strength to come out of all the darkness I have been in for far too long, in the name of Jesus! I pray you would give me eyes to see the plot of the enemy and I pray you would give me a heart of repentance to come out quickly and completely! I also come praying for the help to stop looking for love in other people, finding myself in relationships that are unhealthy and with those who are just as broken as I am. I pray for wholeness and healing in my life. I pray you would cover me, Lord and that you would deliver me from all that I have willingly opened the door to in my life. I ask all of this in Jesus' Holy Name. Amen!

Chapter 10

Destruction of Life Averted; Life Pattern Redirected, Now on Course

"Trust in the LORD with all thine heart; and lean
not unto thine own understanding. In all thy ways
acknowledge him, and he shall direct thy paths."

Proverbs 3:5–6

It's Time to Get Married and Do Things Right

After living with Miho for a couple of years and going
through all that we went through as a result of our
sin, we set a date and made plans to get married. We
decided to get married in our backyard. The wedding

plans were going quite well. We notified our relatives, asked my Miho's uncle who is a minister to marry us, made arrangements for my family and siblings, who all lived out of town to come for the wedding. The day of our wedding was a beautiful event. We had a great time with family and friends and for us, the wedding was stress free. I could not be happier. We were finally in right standing with God. No longer sinning and boy, was that a relief! Unfortunately, the residual effects of what had been done were still playing out in our lives. It was not as bad because we knew we were trying to do what was right in God's eyes. Everything was much easier to cope with, so it appeared.

With our wedding behind us and less stress in our lives, we are both much more relaxed. My dream life was front and center again. Remember, I said earlier I would pick up the dreams again, well, here we go. I still dreamt and saw things in the spirit. I logged each dream as they occurred. It seemed they were coming more frequently now. One night, I dreamt that Miho and I were riding with a man we did not know. He was driving an old Volkswagen and we were going up this hill, which was on a very thin, two-lane road. The driver seemed to be a native of the land we were in and he knew the roads very well. These roads we were on had no railings (safety), and we were traveling very high on what I would call cliffs. I sat in the middle, in-between the driver and my Miho. The driver talked very freely and open with us. It was, for the most part, a very pleasant trip, outside of traveling on roads with no safety railings. Did I mention, I don't like heights?

Once we arrived at our destination, the driver exited the vehicle and approached a lady waiting nearby. I could hear a little of the conversation. When he returned to the vehicle, he states what the woman said "it's done." As we left and traveled back down the hill, I was worried we would have to go back the way we came. That is, through the bumpy and unprotected road, with no safety rails. Get it? Are you getting the metaphor of the bumpy roads with no safety rails? The driver assured me we would not have to go back the way we came. To these words, I replied, "Hallelujah!" He said the way we would go back down the hill would be much easier, and it was. The ride down was very pleasant and smooth as he told us it would be. There were no bumps as we experienced coming up the hill, and looking down the hill, all I saw was green pastures beneath us. So much so that I was unware of whether or not there were rails on the road. I was so taken with the beauty of the pasture. When we made it down the hill, to the flat land, the dream transitioned to where I was handing my marriage certificate to my HR department at work, so they could change my name.

I knew what God was revealing to me that there were many bumps in the road. Bumps that we created, and once we got ourselves in order, our lives would be much smoother. Miho and I had some lingering issues to work out with our "marriage." In this dream, the Lord was letting us know that what we needed was going to happen suddenly and effortlessly. And it did. Shortly after the dream, our marital issues were resolved. It would not be long before we were able to obtain our marriage license. Some years earlier, when we had our ceremony, there were some legal hang-ups we were informed of by the attorney handling his divorce case. We were told we would have everything in time for our wedding, so we proceeded with the ceremony. Well, within two weeks of our wedding, we did not have the documents as we were told we would. After consulting with those we trusted, we were told this type of thing was common, so it was no big deal and we proceeded with the wedding. How crazy is that statement? I know now, looking back that was clearly out of order!

We Christians and children of God have picked up the bad habit of compromising. I believe I went along with this because I so desperately wanted to be right with God. I know, I know, how is this right with God? I am being honest here, so should you the readers find yourself here—don't do this either! Wait until you have your marriage license in hand and then proceed with a "legal" wedding ceremony. This process took surprisingly longer than either of us wanted. You want to know why it took so long? Two weeks prior to the wedding date, the Lord told me to postpone the wedding. Huh? I had already sent the invitations out. Pride! What would I tell all of our guest? Pride! What would I tell my family who had already made travel plans? Pride! How would I explain to my entire guest list, we were going to have to postpone and a new invitation would be sent out? Pride! I am telling you, do things right in your life and AVOID all of the unnecessary problems that come with being out of God's order! It would be a much longer time than either of us wanted, but we were able to get our legal issues resolved and we are legally married. Praise God. I am happy to assert, we are Mr. and Mrs. Carl Lee Abram, Jr. and we are in Godly divine order. Thank you, Jesus!

SIDE BAR: *Now being married to my husband, my confidant and my biggest cheerleader, my Miho, Mr. Carl Lee Abram, Jr., I would be lying if I told there was no residue from the decisions we made. But God has been merciful towards us. A lot of people think when you disobey God and you repent, that it automatically releases you from the consequences of your actions. Repentance means to turn away from your sin and turn back to God. However,* *that does not necessarily However, that does not necessarily mean you will not experience the repercussions of your decisions. If you drop a glass and proceed to step in the path of the glass before "cleaning" it up, you will inevitably get cut, Hello somebody! Now God can choose to show mercy on who he chooses to show mercy. For the next few years, we would go through some pretty hefty struggles, but we made it. Bless God!*

I Know Who I Am

Together with God, we have triumphed over some very steep hurdles and still we stand, solid and committed to each other as ever. I will not lie and tell you there has not been times when we wanted to walk away. The stress of it all took an amazing toll on us. I have learned from my last marriage how to truly fight for my marriage. I've learned how to go before God in prayer and in fasting. Does this mean it doesn't get hard at times? Absolutely not; it does get hard and sometimes extremely hard. My beloved sisters, please know this: the harder you fight, the more things will appear to go totally haywire, but trust me, God is working in the background. **Do Not** surrender to your emotions and start reacting in your feelings. That is an absolute no, no! Stay in the spirit. Remember earlier I said you cannot handle a spiritual issue in a natural way? You can't! As my sister in Christ, Prophetess Alicia would say "Stay on the wall."

SIDE BAR: *When you are fighting for your marriage, there will be a host of outside influences, especially from those who love you. In an effort to help you, they will not always agree with your choices. You will have to be careful who you share your marital struggles with. Some may not understand how to "stand in the gap" in prayer. To them, it may look like you're wasting your time; fighting a fight that is not worth the effort. To that, I would say this, "Was the effort Jesus made for us worth it?" Follow God's instructions and always remember the mercy that was shown to you and trust God to extend the same to your spouse. Like someone no doubt did for you and me, else we may not be here today. We must the same for them.*

Now, if you're in an abusive marriage, in any manner, seriously seek God for direction and do as he instructs.

Never before have I known what it meant to really be loved until now. This is because previously, I did not know how to accept the love of God that was offered through Jesus Christ. Today, I can honestly tell you I know who I am, because I know whose I am. I now know all I had been through was not, and is not today, nor will it ever be a determining factor in who I am in Christ Jesus. It was merely the means to my coming into my destiny and my purpose. It may not have been the ideal way God desired it; however, in the end, it served its purpose. Hallelujah!

You may be asking, "why did your life have to go as it did?" Believe me, there was a point in my life where I was asking that exact same question. I no longer ask that question. Today, I thank God because I have now begun to see the purpose and there is nothing, nothing but praise on my tongue for my Lord and my Savior! Yes, I have come to understand what it truly means to be saved, to be redeemed, to be restored, to be forgiven, to be given mercy and to be shown compassion. Today, I know what it is to have a Lord, my sweet Lord. Yes, I am walking in the favor of my God according to Isaiah 61:1–3 *"The Spirit of the Lord GOD is upon me; because the LORD hath anointed me to preach good tidings unto the meek; he hath sent me to bind up the brokenhearted, to proclaim liberty to the captives, and the opening of the prison to them that are bound; to proclaim the acceptable year of the LORD, and the day of vengeance of our God; to comfort all that mourn; to appoint unto them that mourn in Zion, to give unto them beauty for ashes, the oil of joy for mourning, the garment of praise for the spirit of heaviness; that they might be called trees of righteousness, the planting of the LORD, that he might be glorified."* God has given me beauty for ashes, how sweet my savior!

His Ever So Freely Given Mercy Towards Me

Through it all, I have learned and accepted that I have no grounds to ask God "why?" He is God in it and through it all. What I can do is be grateful that like with Jesus and all other believers, God has never once left or forsaken me. These are not just words taken from the bible, I have lived these words and I know them to be certain! He has shown me time and time again his unfailing love. He has revealed to me on more than one occasion, his kindness and his freely given mercy. He has given me more reasons than not to love him and to praise him. We may not always like our life's journey. We may regret our past decisions and choices. We may dislike the choices and the wicked natures of others. Regardless of how we came to be or what our experiences have been, God is still God, he reigns supreme and he has a great purpose for your life!

When we come to a place of total surrender and trust in God, all things really do work together for the good. Today, I not only know who I am, but I know what I was called and created to do. Like that Hollywood star I was so upset with, I now understand what it is to really breathe life, to live life, to have real and true purpose. To have a renewed compassion for mankind that is not motivated and driven by my own selfish desires. Had I never experienced hardship and pain, I would not have come to know the depths of God's love so intimately. I would have never come to me, my true "authentic" self. For the first time, I like me and I'm happy being me! Knowing, accepting and being happy with the truth has made this not-so-easy journey, a journey I've come to love and appreciate. I realize the benefits have far out-weighed the challenges I endured. I contently believe my life's purpose has really just begun! Today, I truly trust God and that does not come without challenges, but I'm willing to trust him in and through them all! The process of overcoming will always be an ongoing process so long as we live and breathe.

Back in Chapter One

Remember the subtitle *"Through the Blood of Jesus"* in chapter one? I said it seems as though my life had been in some sort of wild whirlwind with many ups, downs, shifts, and changes in-between. I continued to say, it would be October of 2014 when yet another one would come, and that was the shift with caring for my grandmother? This was the final test in our overcoming this period of our lives. With all that occurred, I just did not know if we could take another shift or blow. Praise God we made it through. This was the test that would personally prove my ability to "hold" the word of God, with many things coming against me at the same time. Remember, Joseph had to "hold" the word of God through being sold, enslaved, accused of sexual assault, and imprisoned? We were being hit with all kinds of spiritual attacks and from every possible direction. Only three people really knew what was going on in our lives. You name it, it was happening to us. However, these attack had a different spirit behind them than the attacks before we were married. But, they seemed to be just as painful. Perhaps, because things were no longer out of order where we were concerned. Things were moving and doors were opening, but we still had struggles. We encountered several financial struggles and I had NEVER gone through anything like this one before. We lost three cars and I had NEVER lost a car in my life! Our credit scores took a SERIOUS nosedive! We were struggling to pay the basic household bills and to buy food.

It was so bad I remember going to the local welfare office to get a box of food. I remember crying as I sat in the car they were looking for to repossess, deciding whether or not I was going to go into the welfare office. I went looking for financial help. The woman I spoke to made me feel worthless! The manner in which she looked at me and the imposing questions she asked made me feel violated. I remember thinking, "if this is what single women and single mother's go through just to get help, I've got to help them." She handed me a packet of information (about 30+ pages) to fill out and return, telling me to wait while she went and got a box of food for me. When she handed me the food, I looked at the box and from what I could see, the food was only a day short of going bad. I thought to myself, "WOW!" I dried the tears from my face, pulled my beanie down on my head and headed out the door, hoping and praying the car was still there. I had never sought any kind of government assistance since I lived with my mother and I was a teenager then. I had hit an all-time low and this was uncomfortable. I mean things were so bad, (my Lord they were bad). Through it all, God kept us! You hear me, HE KEPT US!

All of what I told you about above occurred over a three-year period, and despite what was going on, I continued to help the women who were calling me, even when I had to dry my tears to encourage them through theirs. Praise HIM! I still accepted request to participate on prayer calls and minister, even when I felt like it was me that needed to be ministered too! Praise HIM! I continued through and hosted the first women's conference not knowing how we were going to pay our rent. Praise HIM! We continued hosting the SPF-90 Day Encouragement Program at the nonprofit, supporting young women and single mothers. Praise HIM! We still gave out 200 FREE Easter Baskets to kids in our community, when we did not know how we were going to eat. Praise HIM! We held our 2nd Annual Women's conference

right smack in the middle of me caring for my grandmother, with no sleep, no help, back pain, and heavy
financial struggles. Praise HIM! I still posted encourage-
ments on Facebook as God gave them to me, when all
hell was breaking lose all around me and no one knew,
Praise HIM! And, I was still able to FINISH this book,
with ALL OF THAT GOING ON, Praise HIM!

I could not have done ANY of this without those faithful
ones whom God sent as a support, and a blessing to me!
First, my husband, who could have walked out a long
time ago, but he stayed. And, I can't tell you how many
times he would tell me, he saw God keeping us. And
things were going to get better. To keep doing what I was
doing and that he had my back! All that was going on, I
was not alone. This was God-ordained, a collective effort
and God was showing me how to trust him, despite the
circumstances! To keep moving with him even though
it was looking real strange and I was taking all kinds of
slack from folks, including those in my family, which
hurt! It was God and God alone who sent the support
and got us all through this season that is now over. God

does not need a lot of people to do a great thing; he sent eight faithful people and for each of them, I am forever grateful! You know who you are!

Where Is Your God Now?

In 2011, God gave me a dream that I was dressed as a bag lady. I was looking pretty awful and dirty. I was walking down the streets of New York, in-between what was like a soul train line and there were people on both sides of me. They were yelling things like "where is your God now?" "Why aren't you dressing like you used to?" They were mocking me as I walked through the line, appearing to be afraid of them. They seemed like they were going to hurt me because they were so rowdy. When I looked up between two buildings ahead of me and I saw the sun shining through, I woke up to these words "In the end, I will glorify myself." Waking up to these words, eased the fear of the dream, but I truly did not have a clue what the dream would entail. A few weeks or so before that dream, I was sitting at my computer working when Donnie McClurkin's song "Trust" begin to resonate in my spirit and without hesitation, I responded, "uh oh." I knew I was about to go through something. I just did not know the extent, or how bad it would be. Once again, to God be the Glory, we made it!

Just like a loving Father, God would come to encourage our spirits and it would be in October of 2015 when the Lord said "We made it." I just started screaming and shouting all through the house. I didn't need to know what we made it through, just to know we made it was enough for me. Praise God! A few days later, he said I passed the Abraham and Isaac moment and again, I just shouted and screamed, and this time I cried! He explained what that meant and it was all praise from there!

Had I not pushed through EVERYTHING that was going on and continued on with the things God had given, I would have missed the blessing of being informed in January 2011, by the Bishop of the church we attended, that I had an Apostolic Call on my life. I would not have been anointed by Prophetess Alicia Brown as a

Prophetess of God on June 28, 2014. I would not have been licensed as a Minister by our Pastor, Pastor Donald A. Jackson, Jr. on September 30, 2015. I am now doing the will of God, the purpose in which I was sent. Sister's Celebrating Each Other, Inc. the nonprofit God has given me was officially incorporated in the State of California on August 23, 2011 and we are currently planning our 3rd annual women's conference, our 3rd Annual Easter Basket Give Away, our 3rd Annual Clothing Drive, our 4th Annual Holiday Gift Giving Campaign and our first Annual Vision Launch Gala. God has opened doors for us to partner with local government agencies in support of assisting women and their children. We have been offered the opportunity to share the programs God had given me back in 2011 with other nonprofits who support women and children. I published the first of seven book titles God has giving me. You are reading now.

I have started touring to share my story through what we are calling the Victory Tours. Our clothing line will be debuting soon, the speaking engagements have begun and so much more. God is truly doing as he said he would. He is indeed glorifying himself!

Who Changed the Truth of God into A Lie?

God interrupted my "so-called" life and put me on course to fulfill the will and the purpose he created for me. Perhaps, I would not have had to go through some of the pain, hardship and heartache I went through had I not been resisting God's nudging. Resisting the pull was really an act of rebellion. I was as those Paul was writing to in Roman's 1:25, I had chosen unrighteousness over righteousness and in doing so, I did as the scripture states, "changed the truth into a lie". . . Remember, I knew God before I committed adultery and started down a road of total and complete sin. I had a pretty healthy relationship with him. He had made himself very known to me. I made a choice and tried to use my sad, pity party and "woe is me" mindset to justify my wrong doing. When God began to redirect my life, it was not an easy journey for me. I had to unload a lot of the stuff I had picked up along the way, and can I tell you, I had a lot of baggage to unload.

Through everything, God has been faithful to me. It's because of my experiences that I want to help women—young and mature alike. I want them to know their self-worth and who they are in Christ, so they do not end up settling for less than what their heavenly Father has pre-destined for them. I desire to help them avoid the pitfalls I ended up in. It's because of my own experiences that I want to speak to and assist young women and mature women alike, and encourage them in overcoming. It's because of what I went through as a young adult that I want to help young women find and know their purposes in life and help them to avoid unnecessary struggles and heartache. It because of my own experiences of making decisions that were not God's will that I want to encourage women to seek God and to be ensured they are making Godly choices; being led by the Holy Spirit, as opposed to their own feelings, desires, wants and needs.

It's because of my own experiences with being barren that I want to speak to women and inform them that they can still find hope and happiness and fulfillment in life, regardless of whether or not they've given birth. It's because of my own experiences with adultery that I am speaking out and encouraging women not to enter into these types of relationships. It's because of my own experiences that I am so passionate about helping women from all walks of life and letting them know of a God who **SO LOVES** them and there is nothing they can do to be separated from his love—NOTHING. According to his word in Romans 8:31–39, *"What shall we then say to these things? If God be for us, who can be against us? He that spared not his own Son, but delivered him up for us all, how shall he not with him also freely give us all things? Who shall lay any thing to the charge of God's elect? It is God that justifieth. Who is he that condemneth? It is Christ that died, yea rather, that is risen again, who is even at the right hand of God, who also maketh intercession for us. Who shall separate us from the love of Christ? shall tribulation, or distress, or persecution, or famine, or nakedness, or peril, or sword? As it is written, For thy sake we are killed all the day long; we are accounted as sheep for the slaughter. Nay,* *in all these things we are more than conquerors through him that loved us. For I am persuaded, that neither death, nor life, nor angels, nor principalities, nor powers, nor things present, nor things to come, nor height, nor depth, nor any other creature, shall be able to separate us from the love of God, which is in Christ Jesus our Lord."*

Prior to my own experiences, I would not have been able to relate, have compassion, or be so passionate about these things. All of my life I had been searching for who I was and what I wanted out of life. Trying to fill what felt like a void in my life. I am happy to announce that the search is over—I know who I am! My life now has purpose. I am fulfilled and my joy is complete in my Lord and My Savior!

Open Up and Be Free

In bringing "I Know It Was the Blood: A Story of Overcoming" to a close, I want to leave you, my readers, with this: secrets are like toxins, they poison you and leave you for dead. The enemy wants us to hide behind our past, coward underneath the fear of judgement and rejection. In doing so, he leads us smoothly into bondage. Have you ever thought about what the word "testify" means? What the word "truth" means? The liberty that is found in both?

Many of us grew up believing and bound by this statement "what goes on in this house stays in this house." I know, I'm going to step on a whole lot of people's family traditions, including my own, but for many, it's that mindset that has paved the way for a lot of women and people in general to suffer in silence. That silence brings forth a whole other set of issues and unfortunately, that belief system is a poisonous legacy that is passed down from generation to generation.

Openly sharing your testimony, the truth of what God has done in your life, is a powerful testament of who he is and of what he offers. It's no wonder we are being attacked in an effort to prevent us from glorifying him. Have we ever given thought to what the enemy is after when he attacks us? Believe me, it's not about you. It's about the God in you, which is the Word of God in you, the purpose of God in you, the promise of God in you. What is it we think he's "attempting" to kill, steal, and destroy?

As God leads, share what he alone has done in your lives. Encourage another sister, or person for that matter and let them know God is real. Jesus is real! The cross is real and the BLOOD and its POWER ARE REAL! The world will never know if we continue to keep our mouths closed.

Your power in overcoming is through the Blood of Jesus Christ! Revelations 12:11, states *"And they overcame him, first by the blood of the lamb, and by the words of their testimony and they loved not their own lives even unto death."* God has given each of us a powerful testimony. Don't let the enemy rob you of your victory, by holding your testimony back out of fear, guilt and shame! If God brought you through it, give Him the glory and share your story! Therein lies your overcoming power! I pray you have been blessed and enlightened as you have read my story of overcoming. God is faithful. If he did it for me, he will do it for you too!

My Psalm of Praise–Psalm 145 (KJV)

I will extol thee, my God, O king; and I will bless thy name for ever and ever. Every day will I bless thee; and I will praise thy name for ever and ever. Great is the LORD, and greatly to be praised; and his greatness is unsearchable. One generation shall praise thy works to another, and shall declare thy mighty acts. I will speak of the glorious honour of thy majesty, and of thy wondrous works.

And men shall speak of the might of thy terrible acts: and I will declare thy greatness. They shall abundantly utter the memory of thy great goodness, and shall sing of thy righteousness. The LORD is gracious, and full of compassion; slow to anger, and of great mercy. The LORD is good to all: and his tender mercies are over all his works. All thy works shall praise thee, O Lord; and

thy saints shall bless thee.

They shall speak of the glory of thy kingdom, and talk

of thy power; to make known to the sons of men his

mighty acts, and the glorious majesty of his kingdom.

Thy kingdom is an everlasting kingdom, and thy

dominion endureth throughout all generations. The

Lord upholdeth all that fall, and raiseth up all those

that be bowed down. The eyes of all wait upon thee;

and thou givest them their meat in due season.

Thou openest thine hand, and satisfiest the desire of

every living thing. The Lord is righteous in all his ways,

and holy in all his works. The Lord is nigh unto all

them that call upon him, to all that call upon him in

truth. He will fulfil the desire of them that fear him: he

also will hear their cry, and will save them. The Lord

preserveth all them that love him: but all the wicked

will he destroy. My mouth shall speak the praise of

the Lord: and let all flesh bless his holy name for ever

and ever."

Resources and links:

- The Effects Separation and Attachment shared from the Jordan Institute for Families. You can read more on this article on their website at. http://www.practicenotes.org/v012 n04/effects of separation and attachment.htm

- "How Do They Behave" shared from the Australian Government Initiative. You can find this article and more on children and separation at their website at *http://www.familyrelationships. gov.au/BrochuresandPublications/Pages/ ChildrenAndSeparationBooklet.aspx*

- Suppressed Memory—This comes from an article written in the Stanford Report (Stanford University), the article can be found and viewed on their website at http://news.stanford.edu/ news/2004/january14/memory-114.html.

- Adult Survivors of Childhood Trauma—This study/article can be found on the "International Survivors of Childhood Trauma' s website at http://www.istss.org/public-resources/remembering-childhood-trauma.aspx.

- Here is a link with data "Child Trends," this data shares information about the family structure http://www.childtrends. org/?indicators=family-structure

- National Sexual Assault Hotline—You can find out more information on their website at *https:// rainn.org/*

- Alcoholics Anonymous—You can find out more information on their website at *www.aa.org*

- The National Suicide Prevention Lifeline—You can find out more information on their website at *http://www.suicidepreventionlifeline.org/* or call 1–800–273-TALK (8255). This is a 24/7 hotline.

- Mothers Against Drunk Driving—You can find out more information on their website at *http://www.madd.org/* or call 1–800–438–6233.

- The National Child Abuse Hotline—You can find out more information on their website at *https://www.childhelp.org/* or call 1–800–422–4453.

- The National Domestic Violence Hotline—You can find out more information on their website at *http://www.thehotline.org/* or call 1–800–799–7233 or 1–800–787–3224 (TTY).

- National Indigenous Women's Resource Center—You can find out more information on their website at *http://www.niwrc.org/about-us* or call *406–477–3896.*

- The National Runaway Switch Board—You can find out more information on their website at *http://www.1800runaway.org/* or call 1–800–786–2929.

- Parents of Murdered Children—You can find out more information on their website at *http://www.pomc.org/* or call 1–888–818–7662.

- Women's Law —You can find out more information on their website at http://www.womenslaw.org/

- National Association for Infertility—You can find out more information on their website at http://www.resolve.org/

- Divorce Support Center—You can find out more information on their website at http://www.divorcesupportcenter.com/

- On this website there is an interesting article by Ramona W. Denby and Jessica Ayala School of Social Work, University of Nevada Las Vegas, Las Vegas, Nevada, USA—*Am I My Brothers Keeper: Adult Siblings Raising Younger Siblings.*

- Administration for Children and Families—You can find more information on their website at http://www.acf.hhs.gov/

- Child and Family Services Review—You can find more information on their website at http://www.acf.hhs.gov/

- Children's Bureau—You can find out more information on their website at http://www.acf.hhs.gov/programs/cb

- On this website you will find data on "Child Trends." This data shares information about the family structure *http://www.childtrends.org/?indicators=family-structure*

- Daily Strength—http://www.dailystrength.org/

- National Alliance for Grieving Children—The National Alliance for Grieving Children promotes awareness of the needs of children and teens grieving a death and provides education and resources for anyone who wants to support them. Find out more about the NAGC by vising their website at https://childrengrieve.org/about-us

Book/Website Referrals:

Tish Wetzel

(925) 813-0821

http://www.photographybytish.com

Prophetess Alicia Brown

"Wives on the Wall: 365 Prayers and Declarations for Wives to Pray for their Husbands"

"I Am"

http://www.anewministries.com/about.html

www.soulfoodcoach.org

www.armrocks.org

Lori S. Robinson

"I Will Survive: The African-American Guide to Healing from Sexual Assault and Abuse"

http://www.lorirobinson.com/

Pamela Dobson

A Family Affair

http://bookstore.authorhouse.com/Products/SKU-000409455/A-Family-Affair.aspx

Maleeka Eaglin

Living for God and Loving It

http://www.amazon.com/Living - God - Loving - Maleeka -Eaglin /dp/1626970696

Karen D. Lewis

Detour to Strait Street

http://www.detourtostraightstreet.com

Alondra Williams

"The Iron Rose: You've got more metal than you think"

The Burning Rose

Tonya Amos

Happy Feet

52 Weeks of Exercise Inspiration

www.AspirePilatesCenter.com

Mother Rosemary Saffold

God's Team International—Powerful Prayer Line Ministry and more

www.gtnm.org

About the Author

Ceola J. Abram is an entrepreneur, inspirational speaker, and author. She spends her time speaking with groups of women at church events, women's conferences, and other events that encourage and promote unity among women.

Ceola is the founder and Executive Director of Sister's Celebrating Each Other, Inc., a nonprofit organization in Pittsburg, California that supports single women and single mothers. She is the host of Sister's Blog Talk Radio Show "Sister's" and a quarterly panel discussion on YouTube titled "A Sister's Heart."

www.sceoanew.org

The Living Life and Loving It Women's Conference

Is an annual women's conference held in conjunction with Sister's Celebrating Each Other, Inc. in June of each year

Ceola is also the owner of A Gift of Love, LLC

A Gift Basket Business

www.agiftoflovegb.com

Chic Word Wear, LLC

Ceola's new clothing line that is forthcoming

From Female to Woman to Lady

A play Ceola wrote debuting soon

To learn about more about Ceola, please visit

www.ceolajabram.com

Ceola is married to Carl Lee Abram, Jr. and the two make their home in Northern, California

To contact the author write:

CJA Enterprise

C/O Ceola J. Abram

640 Bailey Road, Suite #439

Bay Point, CA 94565

or call 1–800–379–1189

Internet address: *www.ceolajabram.com*

FRONT AND BACK COVER IMAGES BY:

PHOTOGRAPAHY BY TISH

http://www.photographybytish.com

CPSIA information can be obtained at www.ICGtesting.com
Printed in the USA
LVOW10s2002131016

508666LV00010B/25/P